The *Mad Hot* Adventures of an Unlikely Documentary Filmmaker

The *Mad Hot* Adventures of an Unlikely Documentary Filmmaker

AMY SEWELL

Writer and Producer of
mad hot *Ballroom*

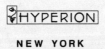

NEW YORK

To my magical daughters, Raquelle and Samantha, who are the light of my life and never cease to amaze me by teaching me something new every day, and who always ask about everything I do, "Mom, are you done yet?" To which I can now reply, "Yes, girls. I'm done . . . with this book."

And to my awesome husband, Charlie, who inspires me to no end with his talents and abilities to coach, teach, and motivate kids, and who is wise enough to never ask if I'm done.

Contents

Acknowledgments

*T*his book would not exist without my editor, Miriam Wenger, whose compassionate yet stealth-like intuition and expertise helped craft it into something so much more. Thank you, Miriam! Thanks to Hyperion's top brass, Ellen Archer, Gretchen Young, and Will Schwalbe, for making it happen. Thanks also to Rita Madrigal, who meticulously copyedited with care, and Laura Drew, who designed the bold and lively cover, and to Paramount Pictures for graciously sharing their artwork.

Thanks to my fabulous agent and friend, Philippa Brophy, and my wonderful lawyer and friend, Roz Lichter—both for believing in me.

Special thanks to my own "in-house" editing team: my sister, Susan Howard, who was my "boredom" barometer ("I took a shower at this part . . .") and helped to keep the book flowing; my mother, Daphne Ottens, who was on top of correcting my grammar for the book (and all my life) and is always able to read what's most important, usually what is intuited between the lines; my father, Richard Ottens, who eliminated my curse words; my mother-in-law, Phyllis Sewell, who made sure I "played nice," even with some of the real rascals on the job, and who loved every draft regardless.

And always, last but never least, thanks to my girrrrlllllfriends for their unwavering support and unconditional love, their reality-check slaps across the face at much needed times, and their always willing participation to discuss anything and everything over a glass of wine: Patty Freud, Barbie "Ulmer" Guest, Catherine Ryan, Susan Toffler, Pam Weadick, and Annie Z.

The *Mad Hot* Adventures of an Unlikely Documentary Filmmaker

Dear Reader,

This is my story of the making of the documentary movie Mad Hot Ballroom. *I am not an expert, per se, not even close. I've made only one movie (but I hope to make more). My goal in writing the book is really to inspire anyone, anywhere, and to show that if you put your mind to something you want to achieve outside the daily realm of who you are and what you do, you can actually do it.*

After all, who would have thought that a stay-at-home mother of twins, with absolutely no filmmaking experience, could go on to make and sell one of the most successful documentaries of all time? Even more important than that, a movie I hear is enjoyed by so many people everywhere.

But it's true. It happened. And that alone should instill hope in anyone who picks up this book that he or she can try to make a documentary film. It's not at all easy, but it's a hundred times more rewarding than one would think. It takes a huge commitment and, while this story is told from my perspective, the making of a documentary does not just happen with one person. It is a collaborative effort of all who are in-

volved and all who contribute a piece of their souls, through talent and hard work, to the overall soul of the film.

And just for the record because I have been asked a million times, I do not ballroom dance. I never have. As I don't have enough time these days to wash my hair let alone learn to cut the rug with a clever foxtrot, I probably never will. I became head-over-heels passionate about a subject I knew nothing and cared nothing about up until I saw the kids dance.

Looking back, I embarked on the journey to make Mad Hot Ballroom *because I found a nugget of a story that made it easy for me to understand, at a time when it seemed the world was going to hell in a handbasket, that life was about affirming the positive. I had reached a point in my life, after witnessing the whole 9/11 tragedy in my own "backyard," when I wanted to change the world for the better. All too often it is through children that we learn the most, and so telling this story seemed the perfect way to start.*

1

The Idea

*I*n February 2003, after freelance writing a couple of columns for a local community paper, the *Tribeca Trib*, the editor asked if I wanted to cover a story about a neighborhood school's fifth-grade students, who take a school-chosen but class-mandatory semester of ballroom dancing instruction. I had turned forty the previous autumn, and was experiencing a fairly early mid-life crisis, pondering what I had done with my life and, more important, wondering what was I going to do with the rest of it. My then five-year-old twin daughters were entering first grade and the chaotic duties of domestic multitasking and childrearing had taken a toll on my mental state and run their course. I knew I had to do something and was anxiously searching for the answer. While my greatest ambition was to write like Anna Quindlen or Nora Ephron, twenty-five years of work and forty years of life had taught me that you always have to start somewhere and that sometimes things come to you as a gift, ever so modestly disguised, it seems, to help jump-start the process—that "new lease on life," as some like to call it.

The commitment to the ballroom story was long (ten weeks, two mornings a week) and the pay low, but something inside me said, Why not? I have been a writer my whole life without ever feeling confident enough to call myself a writer. I wrote my first poem at the age of seven, and four plastic bins under my bed hold what has poured out of me since in the way of poems, short stories, screenplays, and started-but-never-finished novels. While I felt I had paid my dues for years in writing by the number of rejection letters received and submissions never acknowledged, I also knew as a businessperson that nothing worthwhile is easy, nothing is free, and if you want it, you have to work hard for it. This *gift* to write a feature for an editorially well-respected paper presented itself. Not completely thrilled and frankly kind of scared, I felt as if I were twenty again (in all the bad ways); starting new, now at the age of forty, I took the job.

When I attended the first class, I had my notebook out but I could barely write a word. I was mesmerized by the kids and all their expressions; the dance instructor and his hilarious style of instruction; the teacher, with her conscious and unconscious focus on her students; and the dynamic interplay that bounced around the room among all of them. Added to that was the joy of watching kids learn, enjoy a new style of dancing, and, with open arms and open ears, enthusiastically embrace "old" music.

I remember watching the whirl of activity with a keen eye and a sense of excitement that I had stumbled upon something only I could see. I thought, This would make a great movie.

I found the whole concept of these prepubescent kids having to take a course in something as staid and boring (as was the prevalent thinking) as ballroom dancing fascinating. They were at an age when they still wore their emotions on their sleeves—too old to be considered cute and too young to be cool and hip—on the edge of "falling" into the complexities of the world. Kids that age, dancing those dances, didn't seem to fit. They started out afraid to touch and look at one another. They danced so awkwardly in the beginning and even halfway into the course. They never would have chosen to add this class to their already overbooked schedules (typical of many New York City kids and, for that matter, kids everywhere), but they *had* to take it because it was required. It appeared this type of activity would fail before the second class. That didn't happen.

The arc of the story I saw the first year, which was legitimized the next year while filming, is that while there is all this confusion, hesitation, and incompetence in the beginning, these ten- and eleven-year-old children actually end up rising to the occasion and going on to become the little "ladies and gentlemen" ever so subtly expected of them. All the while, they are incorporating manners, courtesy, and respect into their daily dance routines and end up dancing well in a very short period of time. These kids eventually found it to be pretty cool to do something that their parents couldn't do (maybe even their grandparents). They actually got into Frank Sinatra and Peggy Lee—sometimes belting out the words. To me, all of this was wonderful and touching. I couldn't stop thinking about it.

THE TEAM

I knew exactly who I should talk to about my idea for a film. My friend Marilyn Agrelo had worked in film production for ten years, making commercials, industrial and fund-raising films, and film shorts, and had some preliminary footage for a documentary about her family in Cuba. She was born there and came to the United States when she was three years old, her family settling in a suburb just north of the Bronx outside of New York City. She later moved to the city to attend university and then work in public relations and the music industry.

I had met her years before on a double date when she was dating one of my husband's friends. We hit it off immediately and became good friends. During the following years, Marilyn and I made a point of getting together often. Later on, we slowed to meeting only once or twice a year as careers and lives, hers in production and mine in motherhood, kept our reunions to an annual event.

Every time we'd get together, after a glass of red wine or two (okay . . . a bottle), and intrigued by what she did professionally, I'd always say, "Marilyn, let's make a movie together."

She would politely entertain me with the question, "About what?"

To which I'd reply, "I don't know. . . . Let's think of something."

And then, as if she had said it a thousand times to everyone and anyone who ever pitched her an idea, she'd reply with a sigh, "Well, when you have that idea, give me a call."

In mid-July 2003, my husband, Charlie, and I were away for a weekend and we were having one of those review-of-our-lives discussions that all married couples have, or at least I think they have. Do we like where we are living? How are our kids doing? Do we need a new car? When is he going to get around to cleaning up his piles and piles of stuff? Are we happy? What's up with our careers, our jobs? Having just finished the article and feeling very satisfied about it, I said to him, "I'm going to make a documentary about kids ballroom dancing in the New York public schools." I had told him that I'd had a vision while reporting and felt that I could pick up a couple books, figure it out, and do it. He simply replied, "You go, babe."

He wasn't surprised and he certainly knew about the cloth from which we were both cut—the do-it-yourself kind—as starting from scratch is what he had done both in his teaching and coaching careers. I then bought a book about writing, directing, and producing your own documentary and read it. After taking some notes, I lay back on the couch, shut my eyes, and tried to envision the movie I would like to see about the subject. When I woke up two hours later, I sat down at the table and wrote an outline of the movie I saw in my mind. Once I did this, I thought, Now what? I decided that it was no fun to work alone and that I really needed the help of someone who had experience in the world of production.

And like a lightbulb flash, I thought, Of course . . . Marilyn. We always wanted to make a movie together! Added to that, I knew no one else in the world of production. It was really a no-brainer.

*M*y article about the kids ballroom dancing was published in late July 2003. On August 1, I called Marilyn and said, "I have that idea." Because she was the logical and only choice as a partner, I never thought twice about it. It's like hitting a golf or tennis ball—when you hit it right, it's effortless. That's how this partnership felt. I had no internal struggle about taking this to the next level; I just leaped. I think when you do things like this, the more you think about it, the more likely you are to talk yourself out of it. I wasn't going there. Having a mid-life crisis is always an effective way to give you a good shove too.

Marilyn says that throughout her career, she's worked on a wide variety of projects, but she had never imagined making a film about children, let alone children dancing. I, on the other hand, have always imagined myself doing all sorts of things, and so, with great passion and energy, throwing all caution, as well as common sense, to the wind, I dived headfirst into an industry of which I knew nothing. And in this crazy kind of way, Marilyn and I seemed to make the perfect match. We brought forth in each other an unbridled enthusiasm and a plethora of thoughts and ideas about our topic. We discussed everything all the time. What she did over and above this as the director, with a fine sense of precision, was capture all our ideas and energy and guide them into a filmmaking vision. This type of energy and motivation continued through the whole life of the project.

*I*n August, I invited Marilyn over to discuss the concept in more detail. She came with her partner, Brian David Cange, who is also a filmmaker. With Marilyn and Brian situated comfortably on the couch, and with a glass of red wine no less, I laid out my arsenal: four documents—the outline I devised from the helpful book I read, a pitch letter with support documents for fund-raising, an ambitious action plan, and a list of film festivals to which I wanted to submit our yet-to-be-made movie. The action plan was a serious tool to me then but when I look back, it's funny how I prioritized things that wouldn't need to be addressed until *after* we had a product. The fund-raising letter was as sappy as you can get, but it got across the vision and certainly brought forth my passion. My philosophy was to know no boundaries.

I gave them the pitch and looked at them both with great anticipation. They just sat there. For a moment, I thought that I hadn't gotten my point across correctly. I couldn't understand why they weren't showing the same excitement I was feeling about it all. I remember Brian saying he was impressed with the "homework"—the documents. It was kind of a crazy idea from someone who not only had never made a movie before, but who also had no experience in film and video production. We continued to talk about it well into the night.

When Marilyn and Brian left, I watched them quietly walk to my elevator. I had no idea whether Marilyn was interested or not. They told me later that Brian got into the elevator, looked at Marilyn, and said, "Make sure you want to do this . . . and if you don't, make sure you let her down easy. She's pretty excited about this dancing kid thing." They walked quietly to the subway to go home. When Marilyn called me the next day and told me she would make the movie with me, I literally jumped with joy. I was enthusiastic about working with her.

We ended up having great respect for each other—respect for how differently our minds processed things or calculated situations. What might have been nicest of all is that we often addressed things in very different ways, forcing each other to see another perspective, which was continuously refreshing. Marilyn has always said that she likes to hold her cards close to her chest. She is not one to lay it all out. I, on the other hand, wear it all on the outside. I have always felt like I have nothing to lose, and so those who know me know that they get the whole ball of wax—the emotional, mental, physical, and intellectual coming at them all at once. This kind of relationship— business partnership—ended up being a real positive in the development of the project. We were into pushing limits—our own and each other's.

I told Marilyn two things that night she called to say she would do it. The first was that I had worked very hard my whole life (sometimes working as many as three jobs at one time), so I didn't want to work that hard. She too had put in the hours in her industry, an industry that is neither easy nor flexible. I remember Marilyn once saying, "Tears are not an option in production."

The schedule, I thought then, also had to fit my needs. I was relieved that we'd be shooting mostly during school hours—I had kids to get to school and pick up and I didn't have hired help. I was looking to make it all work out. The second thing I told Marilyn was that our goal, regardless of everything and anything, at our age, should be just to have some fun.

What we didn't realize at the time is that we would never work harder in our lives, that the schedule I thought would fit my needs changed along the way to become very demanding and brutal, and that we would shed some tears at times. And to this day, we are still saying, exhausted and out of breath, "Are we having fun yet?"

ACTION PLAN

1. Find a great idea (or one you think is a great idea, and ignore everyone who tells you you're crazy).

2. Find a good partner (easier said than done, but think long and hard and find a complement, not a clone). If you are coming in with absolutely no experience, it is best to find someone who has worked in production. If you are lacking a business background, you might do best bringing in a third partner with expertise in this area.

3. Create an outline of your movie. Even though it is a documentary, there is a vision of how you see it unfolding before you on the screen. Write that "unfolding" down, the possible scenes that you envision, and use this as a blueprint to follow or from which to deviate. If

this creative process warrants it, you may start to write notes next to the scenes that could end up being the beginning of the narration development if the movie is to be narrated.

4. Create the pitch letter for fund-raising. This will continue to be honed depending on where you are seeking funds, but it will be your template on why you think anyone should give you money for your project.

5. Create an action plan of all the steps you think will be necessary from the very beginning to the very end. Start the action plan while reading this book and take notes of all the action plan points at the end of each chapter.

6. As your carrot, create a list of film festivals you'd like to attend.

7. Leap!

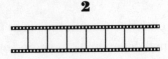

The Film Concept

I had written the article in the spring after following one fifth-grade class in a public school in TriBeCa, located in lower Manhattan. TriBeCa is a neighborhood known for its conversion from a haven for artists in the sixties and seventies to the upscale, trendy place it is today. The school is special because it has only one class per grade, making it particularly cozy and quaint, but it also has some wacky traits because of this insularity. The fact that this warm and fuzzy school is in the middle of one of the biggest, sometimes nastiest, toughest cities in the world is always a bit of a conundrum to me, but it makes for great subject matter.

The documentary in my head at the time was driven by American Ballroom Theater (ABrT), its two codirectors, its stable of teaching artists, and this one little school. I had intended to show the beginning, middle, and final products of the program, and the arc of the story captured in the article. This school happens to be a stone's throw from where I live and close to my daughters' school, where I'd be dropping them off and picking them up daily. It was also extremely convenient should there be that horrible catastrophe a mother is always imagining—you know, a head cracking open at recess or a finger getting slammed in a door and falling off, or, by chance, another horrific terrorist attack. At that time the dirty-bomb-shipping-container threat was hovering over Manhattan. So the whole idea seemed very manageable.

New York City–based American Ballroom Theater is the nonprofit organization that provides ballroom dancing instruction to a small percentage of New York City public schools through their youth-oriented program, Dancing Classrooms. The program was introduced in two schools back in 1994; when we began the documentary, it was in about sixty public schools in New York City.

In half a semester, the kids absorb a repertoire that includes the merengue, foxtrot, rumba, tango, swing, waltz, heel-toe polka, and a couple of line dances, which are thrown in just for fun. The typical eleven-year-old kids become little "ladies and gentlemen," a metamorphosis brought about not only by their determined-to-be-eloquent ballroom dancing execution but also by the main attributes the course espouses—courtesy, manners, and respect.

The ABrT codirectors, Pierre Dulaine and Yvonne Marceau, are the Fred and Ginger of our time. Pierre still holds his statuesque physique in a stately manner, even though his hair is icy white, making him look perhaps even more distinguished. Yvonne is just sheer grace in one long, petite, willowy dose; she reminds those of us who built our cardio bodies in the eighties what a lady truly looks like. They are one of those couples whom you constantly look at in the picture on their studio wall, in the heyday of their youth and at the height of their careers, and then look back at them across the table, now in the fall season of their lives, and think, Wow. They look great. If only I could be so lucky.

Their career highlights are too numerous to list, but include ballroom dancing world championships; choreography for feature films; teaching accolades with Alvin Ailey, the Juilliard School, and the School of American Ballet; *and* lead dance roles on Broadway—most significantly, the featured artists in the 1980s smash show *Grand Hotel*. Yvonne, like a silk scarf, slid down and around the silhouette of Pierre, in an amazing adagio (which is a dance to slow music; also, part of the classical ballet pas de deux). This scene is revered by all who saw it and remembered in the dance world as a transcendent moment.

Dulaine and Marceau's tireless tour de force of introducing and maintaining ballroom dancing in the New York City public school system comes directly from their hearts. This was evident when I first met them while writing the article. They care most about seeing young people understand one another better through the example of ballroom dance and its basic, solid framework, which is deeply entrenched in the concept of good manners. They do it for the love of those kids, because there isn't enough time in a day to make any money from it. And with fiercely loyal teaching artists, they've managed to build a great teaching institution.

*M*arilyn and I had our minds set to have the documentary follow the three-month journey of a New York City public school fifth-grade class into the world of ballroom dancing. From the first steps to a final citywide competition, these kids, some of whom had never danced with another person, would perform the merengue, rumba, tango, foxtrot, and swing, with great precision and verve, and we would document their transformation and all the trials and tribulations.

We anticipated capturing the whole learning experience—the dance lessons morphing from something seemingly simple and quaint into quite a roaring competition, taking on the air of a major sporting exhibition sans the arena. And the viewer would get, in addition, a visual tour of where the competitions are held, the worst, most horribly painted cafeterias and gymnasiums around the city. I expected that because last year's TriBeCa team made it to the semifinals, this year's team would do the same.

The object of winning or losing was never the story to us. It was the journey. We figured the natural drama set forth by depicting these kids, some of whom are in great need of attention and purpose, who would be transformed by mastering something completely out of their realm of experience and daily reality, was entertaining enough. This "fish out of water" experience would make for a good show. And like all kids, they would rise to this opportunity to shine. To be a star—if only for a short time—is a great thing for a kid (and who am I kidding . . . it's great for an adult too).

We wanted the movie, while entertaining, to paint portraits of particular children—at school with their teachers, at home with their parents, backstage, and at the competitions—and to capture as many emotions as possible. At the previous year's semifinal competition, the play of emotions ripped into the hearts of all who were watching. There were times when I was standing on the cafeteria table "taking notes" for the article when I thought I was going to have a heart attack. And these weren't even my kids!

The naïveté and uninhibited enthusiasm of these inner-city kids mixed with the esteemed yet contained world of ballroom dancing would be best portrayed innocently and unpredictably on film. The documentary format made sense because it takes a majority of the senses and puts them right up there in front of you to "feel" and to "taste." Books and newspaper articles will always have words as their limitation, a boundary. Fictionalized television programs or movies have the limitations of one or two writers' imaginations, again bound by words first. There are even historical or factual documentaries, such as *Enron: The Smartest Guys in the Room*, that are written with narration. But a documentary film, one shot vérité, in which we follow the subjects into the unknown, the happenings of real life, has endless opportunities and possibilities. You don't know what you are going to get and with something like dance and kids, it was open to anything. It is this element of the unknown that makes it not only exciting to the filmmakers, but also to the viewers, because the story is presented in just the same way it was experienced when filming. This aspect of surprise can almost be felt, as if in a wave, coming off the big screen. Documentary filmmaking "captures." That is exciting. It is this capturing that makes the medium rewarding to so many, filmmakers and viewers alike.

There are many aspects to explore with bringing something to all the senses to get that feel, that taste. Another was what would be heard. I was a frenzied, excited freak about the music. I saw it serving as a transferential catalyst from one generation to another—and vice versa. The previous year, we had a group of kids who listened to hip-hop or the pop music of today, and once exposed to the "old" music, the girls sang the lyrics to Peggy Lee's "Fever" during class and the boys snapped their fingers to a Sinatra tune long after class was over.

The music was "portaling," coming in through a portal from one space in time to another, from one generation into the next and across cultures. It was cool that white kids who had never heard a rumba tune in their lives were going to sashay across the floor to a song belted out in both style and beat by Lucía Méndez, or fiercely try to move their hips to a merengue with great pizzazz when they heard the rhythm and lyrics of Pochy Familia y Su Cocoband. Or that kids uptown who had been doing the merengue since they were born now had to try to hold still and be poised for the foxtrot or waltz.

I wanted an amazing film soundtrack CD with Peggy and Frank, Pochy and Lucía, Della Reese and Bobby Darin all incorporating a contrasting and highly charged repertoire of songs representative of the days of old to clash with the current "tween" generation's urban taste in music. Music was only a slice of the big picture of what I wanted overall for this film and its purpose.

One day of many that we were discussing, ad nauseam, the vision and strategy, Marilyn, about to head down into the subway, suggested following three or four schools. So while the statement came flying out like an afterthought, it packed all the punch of something that would take this project into another dimension. As I mentioned before, Marilyn is a quiet thinker who keeps it all locked upstairs, but when she comes out with a one-line statement or suggestion, it usually means she has been mulling it over for days, weeks, or longer. She smiled and waved, dark eyes looking right through me, and left me standing there, somewhere on Houston on the Lower East Side, wondering what she had just dropped in my lap.

I remember sighing, because it felt as if this manageable project we had been discussing, with all its contained heart and soul, was starting to grow arms and legs. My goal at this time in my life was to stay small: to write only for the local community paper, to stay quiet, to keep it simple, and to do this little documentary about this small, sweet story. The last thing I wanted to do was put more on my plate than I could handle and set myself up to fail. Following more than one class, especially in the huge monster of a public school system that is New York City, seemed a huge endeavor, in addition to keeping my own kids on course and a household intact.

As I stood there for what seemed like the longest time, digesting what Marilyn had just suggested and trying to weigh it out, in terms of effort and where I was in my life, it hit me, in a New York minute, that she was right. That was the way to tell this story. It was a great idea because the contrast would add depth and texture and present the many different elements that represent the city. She had always thought following only the TriBeCa school was very limiting. This confirmed the direction she wanted to take to bring a richer story to fruition.

What do I really have to lose? I thought. I ran down the subway steps, screaming after her that we had to do it. Marilyn didn't hear me—she had already boarded her train—but hundreds of morning-rush-hour New Yorkers did, much to my embarrassment. Later, when we caught up by phone, I told her it was a wonderful idea, even though I feared the many ways it was growing. This was the first of many discussions about contrast and diversity, which she had often brought up before now, but it was the expansion of adding more schools into the mix that opened up the creative floodgates.

It looked like we had a plan and we were going to pursue it. We started to cast a wide net, discussing how many schools, and within what distance, we'd visit and monitor. We instinctively started to sketch out charts and diagrams with the possible players and the possible movement of the story based on those subjects. We again met with Pierre and Yvonne, who went over each and every one of their schools, talking to us about the "personality" of each school, the classes, the teaching artist in charge, the logistics of location, and the dynamics of the neighborhoods. Of course, we listened almost as intensely to what they were not telling us, which schools they didn't talk about, so we could find out why and see if any of those were of interest. As a writer, it's a learned trait to listen to what's not being said. Sometimes therein lies your story.

We continued to put everything into place and realized we needed a title for our project. Something to call it—a working title. I liked *Not the Same Ol' Song & Dance*, supporting the universal theme of someone new taking on something old. That became our film's working title. Marilyn didn't really care for it.

"Amy," she said, "it will become *Not the Same* on the movie marquees and that won't make sense." I shrugged and sighed. "Details . . . details!" But she smiled at me nonetheless and I smiled back. It was this determined meeting of the minds, if you will, this forced willingness to be open to each other, that carried this project along.

And so along we went—two women, on a mission, not willing to do the same ol' song and dance, and unknowingly destined to become "not the same" people we were when we started out.

ACTION PLAN

1. Fine-tune the outline to include any new information, or new parameters. Documentary filmmaking is about casting a wide net. Define just how big that net will be (even though it may change over time).

2. Start thinking about the big picture. Who is the audience? Who do you want to be the audience? I recom-

mend that you read a basic textbook about product development and marketing.

3. From your definition of the audience, develop a list of goals, including where you see the film ending up—on the big screen or on television (network or specialty cable), and also consider new media outlets such as computers, phones, and text-messaging platforms.

4. Update your action plan.

5. Have a glass of wine with your filmmaking partner, because if you really have a story (and you have a good partner), you are halfway there!

3

The Research

 I had to do my research. I researched everything that went into making a movie and then everything about ballroom dancing.

For a background on ballroom dancing, I hit the New York Public Library for the Performing Arts at Lincoln Center and checked out fifteen books: books on the history of ballroom dancing, books specific to each dance, books about teaching kids to dance, books with foot diagrams—that is, every book available with any mention of ballroom dancing. I even dived into the general history of dance. I got a kick out of learning things that would end up having no importance or relevance to the project, and reaching beyond the informational boundaries I started to establish kept me sane because I enjoyed learning so much more about the topic than would be required. It was enjoyable, like taking a college course in it. For example, I learned that during ancient times, dance was condemned for showing disrespect for all things sacred and for eliciting lustful desires. This kept me going for a couple days.

After I put all this in my head, I went back to the Library for the Performing Arts and watched tapes of dance movies and instructional videos. "Whoa" is all I can say. This type of subject research, for any documentary, is necessary. How else do you find out what may or may not be interesting or worthwhile to shoot? How else do you eliminate the unnecessary? How else do you begin to "see" or find the thread of the story—or in this case, discover exactly what it is you don't want? It was obvious that, fortunately, we'd be filming kids dancing and all this background information would just be filler. A good set of indicators I used then was to continuously ask myself questions: What would I want to see? What would I want to learn? What is interesting to me? Why do I care? I trusted my creative instincts but I also trusted my business instincts. I trusted my taste—as a consumer of movies. What movie would I want to see on this subject? That was the bottom line.

Research makes a vision visible. As a writer, you have to know your subject inside and out. I thought this would apply to documentary filmmaking too. That is what I think of as the core of documentary filmmaking: taking a subject and presenting it so that the audience can learn something new, learn something more interesting about something old, or just be brought into a world to which they wouldn't normally have access. And this barrage of research and information in turn helps to mold and shape your story. Without a story, you have nothing.

Doing the research, starting the project, and then seeing what you get can alter the original vision, either subtly or drastically. My original idea of the opening of the doc had Fred and Ginger dissolving into Yvonne and Pierre as they danced out the door. Back then I wasn't thinking about clearing archival footage and I had no idea that this clip, of maybe six seconds, would cost a lot of money. As I had wanted to include the history of ballroom dancing, obstacles such as cost and, really, depth of information proceeded to shape where the documentary was headed. We first thought, All right, we'd give the viewers a bit of ballroom history and then bring the film's focus to ABrT and its codirectors, Yvonne and Pierre, and the three or four schools we'd follow.

But what was really happening is that certain boundaries such as cost, and certain guidelines such as the importance of a cinematic vision, started to take root. Later, when we began filming, once we had gained the trust of the kids and they began to let it all pour out, both verbally and physically on the dance floor, the story opened up to include more about the kids and less about the adults and the program. What a joy this was. The history of ballroom dance seemed to move farther into the background, but it was good to know it was there to go back to or to think about weaving into the story. The foundation of the information and research was there if it was needed, and it was comforting to know it was all in my head to pull out if need be.

What also became apparent through this step in preproduction was that I had to get a better handle on the filmmaking process and all it entailed. I felt fairly insecure about what I didn't know, but it didn't scare me away. I went to the bookstore and spent a day finding the right books about each step of the filmmaking process (see Appendix B) and I read them. This was my crash course in filmmaking. It certainly wasn't enough—but it had to be, because I didn't have the time to invest in any film classes, let alone film school. I had to go with what I could pick up quickly and what I could learn on my own. Luckily, Marilyn had experience and we would go on to surround ourselves with the right people every step of the way.

I also thought about the worst-case scenario of what I was doing, and if I could live with it, no problem, and if I couldn't, I would change the parameters of what I was about to encounter. I always try to look at the bigger picture about time, space, money, peace of mind, relationships, and how they all relate to the pursuit of a higher quality of life. For example, in my current doc project, I feel that if the best thing that comes out of it is that my daughters and the daughter of my new filmmaking partner become good friends, then that's a great thing. As I've gotten older and watched how things unfold in both the business world and in my personal life, I've noticed that there are definite patterns to what is supposed to happen. I have to say that it is a desirable trait (and a learned one too) to be able to roll with the punches. And in this industry, in any industry for that matter, it is highly advisable. That's not to say I didn't try to maneuver and control as many aspects as possible. It's advisable to do so—to what I would recommend to be a manic level. The important thing is to know when you can't control something anymore, and to let it go. That is the key.

So, of course, I became driven to have a real handle on the business aspects of what I call product development (which is how I thought about this movie—really), and this fit because of my business background. I took the reins in these areas and because Marilyn had to continue to work her production jobs at the time, we discussed things by phone and had as many meetings as we possibly could. Unfortunately, she had also encountered her own personal hardships that fall. I remember telling her that whenever she wanted to raise the white flag and stop, we could. While I told her that I really didn't want to make the movie with anyone else, I also didn't want to tax her. During this time, I made a point to include her only when I really needed her.

Additional research included materials about the market—
the recent success of documentaries, copyright and clearances,
legal issues, possible financial (profit/loss) scenarios, marketing and trending aspects, and how to most effectively raise the
money to make this movie. Every function in product development had to be thoroughly researched.

My huge revelation after five months, after all this research,
was that this was not such a small endeavor. It was huge. Matching my growth of understanding that this would be a very serious
effort was the growth of my passion for what I really wanted this
movie to be. I simply became motivated by a dream—maybe a
little bit delusional—that I really wanted this to be powerful. I
was out to entertain a mass audience in a big way. I remember
thinking, I want to make people laugh and cry—because that is
what *I* like about movies. I wanted to be moved and I wanted to
move others. I wanted to give people that feeling in their hearts,
both heavy and light, and I wanted them to walk out when the
movie was over and not be able to say a word. I wanted people to
really feel the movie and all its aspects—from what it feels like
to be a kid, how important music is to our souls, and how teachers help shape our lives, to how art is the very essence of our be-
ings. I wanted to show how one little program could represent
the importance of offering the arts in education. I wanted to take
something that was educational, that had a message, and deliver
it in a way so that people wouldn't know they were being "told"
the importance of arts in education. Marilyn had talked to me
early on about the idea that we are always overwhelmed by
everything in the world, always being hit over the head, and she
had said that she didn't want to lecture in the film. She wanted to
let people figure it out for themselves. It would be subtle yet
forceful—a perfect combination.

This seemed to be a complete turnabout from what I had originally set out to do, but it wasn't. While originally I had just wanted to tell a small, sweet story, I had never really thought about its reach. Now what we wanted was not so much to just tell a story but to take a "small, sweet story" and make it feel big, play big. To me, the best movies are the little ones, the indie films that come creeping up out of nowhere and grab your mind, heart, and soul. And so what was happening was that we started to think about how to take something that could come off as too educational, or too documentary-like, and make it a project similar to a regular fiction movie that the masses would see. Since I'm a fairly predictable indicator for what is "mass-brow," I kept hold of the movie I had seen in my mind at the very beginning, that had made its way to the outline, which was more entertaining in nature. It also confirmed a belief of mine that, unfortunately, in order to get a point across, something educational, something maybe the masses should see, you have to weave it into something that entertains. Getting the formula of presenting educational material in an entertaining format right was our most important goal, and what helped was always relying on what caught hold of my modern-day, childlike short attention span. And while I may have focused on this to an extreme, more than once Marilyn had voiced her desire to make a work of high artistic merit. Not that I didn't. I certainly did. I just didn't want it to be so traditional in documentary nature and style. But this was perfect. We would end up coming down the pipeline to meet in the middle. We found a formula we both could live with and, while this meeting of two objectives made it all the more challenging, it definitely made it all the more fun.

ACTION PLAN

1. Research. All angles. Everything about the topic. It will bring new ideas to possibly utilize but, more important, it will create boundaries for what you don't want to do. Research also helps to make you think about one idea and how to update it. For example, back in the heyday of ballroom dancing, postwar New York City in all its glory made me think about New York City today, how it's changed, and what it has to offer. What is its glory today and how did that factor into this story?

2. Research and the process of elimination will help you find the core of the story. This helps shape the story. Later, the story may change, but a strong foundation will have been forged from which to investigate going in a new direction or in several new directions.

3. Trust your instincts. Ask the "What . . ." and "Why . . ." questions.

4. Learn about filmmaking—all aspects of it—as best as possible. At least learn what you have to know to hire someone, such as a director of photography who knows all about being a director of photography.

5. Start with reading the list of books recommended in Appendix B.

6. If you don't have a business and marketing background, find a "101" book about that too—and read it.

Or seek out friends in business and ask them questions. In most cases, they will be happy to apply their know-how and ideas to something fun and creative such as filmmaking.

7. Most important, at this point, before you do all the work that lies ahead, make sure you are passionate about your story. Only passion will make you hang on and see it through to the end.

4

Fund-raising

*F*und-raising is neither fun nor easy. I thought there would be absolutely no problem raising the money to make this doc. (Naïveté is great protection.)

We had a good subject, a good "cause" if you will, supporting and showing the importance of the arts in education. Additionally, the popularity of recent contemporary documentaries proved their ability to pull in box office dollars. There hadn't been anything around about ballroom dancing, really, since the popular cult hit *Strictly Ballroom*, which came out in 1992. I knew these things moved in cycles. We were due for another ballroom blitz, so the topic might help prove its worthiness.

And so began the Sisyphean effort of fund-raising, and the large number of letters mailed kept the United States Postal Service from raising their rates for another year and gave *a lot* of corporate donation department executives, industry acquisition executives, and foundation project screeners a good lunchtime read. I didn't know just who might be out there looking for a project like this. I needed only one needle in the haystack.

Before searching for that needle, I needed to have a worthy budget, since I could go in asking for money only once. There's one shot and the budget had to be solid. Suffice it to say that anybody interested in investing needs to see numbers. People who invest money look at numbers. Period. People don't just give money away. To individuals, money is personal. To corporations and foundations, it's all business. And it's a toss-up as to which is worse. Foundations have serious scrutinizing engines, and, like corporations, heavily weigh their investments and/or donations on a cost-reward business model. Corporations have to make a profit, and if my little project was not going to give them worthy returns (measured in money and/or public relations), they would not have "an extra" $10K to throw my way. The budget is a great tool: it has to be included with grant and filmmaking competition applications and it can also be used as a general map in planning the filmmaking tasks that lie ahead. (There is more on the budget in Chapter Seven.)

In asking people, companies, and foundations for money— a lot of money—the last thing I wanted to do was approach with one number and then come back with a larger number later on. After several run-throughs at budgeting the movie, the final number came in at $450,000.

Now, how in the heck do you raise almost half a million dollars without going to a bank or a loan shark?

The very first thing I did was write a holiday letter to friends and family. I wanted everyone to know what I was doing and allow them to get all the jokes and crazy responses out of their systems. I offered them the chance to invest by very simply stating that they could contact me for a business plan. I did this for three reasons: to announce it, so people would know about the movie and could ask me about its status or just go on with their business; to offer people a chance to invest, but by asking *them* to contact *me*, and letting them know that I wouldn't contact them again (making it easy to go to social functions without my friends worrying that I was going to accost them for money if they spoke to me); and, finally, if the movie did happen to take off, to avoid family and friends accosting me with statements like "Why didn't you call me? I would have invested."

Many close to me, even some family members, ignored me. I had come up with many ideas over the years and had done many entrepreneurial things and this was received as another "Amy's up to something" idea. And let's not forget it was about ballroom dancing. The topic doesn't exactly excite many people. I had comments from relatives and certain friends that packed quite a punch of doubt, such as, "Ballroom dancing?????" And, "What do you know about making a documentary?" "What makes you think you can do this?" Really, how do you answer these questions on the spot? The short answer is "I have a brain and I'm going to use it." The long answer wasn't worth the breath. There was too much to do.

Other friends and family members stepped up to the plate in both big and small ways and every bit helped. The greatest chunk of investment came from the three matriarchs in my life: my mother-in-law, her sister, and my mother. My closest friends offered to watch my kids on shoot days. I had a support system from those who mattered. Charlie, my husband, was and still is my biggest fan and my most grounded pillar of support. It doesn't come unconditionally or easy. He's not one to tolerate dummies. All aspects were discussed with him and we had lively, sometimes heated, discussions about strategy, money, legal issues, people, everything. Even my daughters were fans. It was hard for them to let me go to work on this "other baby," the movie. You can't do something like this without surrounding yourself with people who believe in you. (And you have to get rid of all those people who don't—or at least put them aside for a while. Negative energy is just that and will hinder your drive and shake your confidence.)

So once the circle of family and friends were informed and given an opportunity to invest or politely ignore the request for money, I had to build what I called the sales kit because, after all, I was basically selling a concept of what would hopefully be a movie. I have always been in awe of this stage of the sales task simply because you are really selling air. It is just an idea and not only are you selling the idea, you are selling what this idea is to become. All of this is conditional on so many factors. I often equate filmmaking to the game of KerPlunk! You have all these sticks holding up all these marbles and it takes only one pulled stick to make all the marbles drop and come pouring out. With so many aspects and functions coming together to make a movie, it takes only one bad thing happening, one "off" day, to unleash catastrophe in the process. But you can't think about it, or you won't do it.

The sales kit contained a business plan, our movie's budget, the synopsis, and the crew biographies. It also included articles about ballroom dancing and about documentaries with box-office success. Michael Moore's documentaries and Jeffrey Blitz's *Spellbound* had really knocked down some walls around how docs were perceived in the market. And then Morgan Spurlock's successful *Super Size Me*, released in 2004, swung the doors wide open and theatrically released documentaries moved into quite a respectable position within the industry. It was my studying of this trend, more than anything, that convinced me that the time for docs was now, and I used this business information as a primary selling tool to individuals.

Think beyond the basics of what you believe should go into

the sales kit. Include anything that might help sell the concept. Be selective too. I have seen some sales kits so overloaded with information that I can't imagine someone wanting to even start to read anything in them. I know I'm turned off by too much information. Also, not everyone is impressed if you have a major name tied to your project. In fact, sometimes this can backfire if you are seeking smaller investors. They might think that since you have such big-name contacts, you should get the money from that person and his or her friends. They have it, others will think. So, be careful what you put out there and how it might be interpreted. The fact is, the one thing that makes a sales kit stand out is when the reader can feel the passion behind the project.

To seek money from foundations is like "get down and give me twenty" multiplied to infinity. I researched which foundations gave money geared toward projects in dance or film or both. I found Web sites related to similar areas: dance companies, film organizations, and other arts in education programs. I looked at and printed out their lists of contributors—these ranged from foundations and corporations to individuals. Here was my target investor audience. I even went to fund-raisers, brought home the programs, and took a highlighter to contacts I would pursue. Donors tend to donate money to similar organizations with similar objectives. For example, you will find that a person or corporation that has an interest in the arts and/or dance will often give to several organizations within that area.

I didn't apply to foundations that didn't cover our subject area or hadn't already given to even a subset of my subject within the last five years. Most foundations have Web sites, and I read their requirements and also found out who and what type of projects were awarded grants over the past years. The grant strategies are set a year or more in advance and these foundations stick to plan. They are run by managers who in turn usually report to a large board of directors, who are usually very busy and important people in business and elsewhere. To get this group together is hard enough. Once they decide on a course of action, it holds firm.

When I saw a fit, I got an application. The bigger the foundation, the bigger the application. The guidelines and rules were half the application. I freaked out for a moment, because I thought, Who in their right mind has the time to do this? I knew there were people out there who write grants or who specialize in applying for grants, but it was just me, and we were on a budget. I just thought there had to be an easier way.

I had taken a grant-writing course a long time ago. I ended up taking quite a bit of time bringing myself up to date by researching grant writing on the Internet, and also looking into a weekend course. I ended up consulting with a couple of friends who do grant writing for a living, and they felt that with my MBA to back me, I could possibly swing it. I found it to be pretty commonsensical. I filled out the applications—following the directions *meticulously*—and tried to tell them, brilliantly, passionately, and concisely, why they should give our project the money over someone else's.

However, we were already at a disadvantage for getting any grants. Foundations tend to be academic-focused. They fulfill a need and duty in society to uphold and communicate their mission, to put forth the purpose of the foundation's philosophy and impact on their chosen relevant social issues. They like everything supported with facts, statistics, and measurements. Our movie was certainly not going to be academic-heavy. The filmmakers were not and still are not academics (although there have been times each of us has been known to think we know an awful lot about something or other!).

Foundations also have critical deadlines, and usually the application approval process takes months. Even if we did come close to getting any grants (which we did, on a few), the money wouldn't come through, most likely, until six months later. Most grants also asked for follow-up reports and measurements of effectiveness. I was also never quite sure if a providing foundation would have any say in the creative process or final outcome of any film or project—and that was not up for the offering.

I don't want to oversimplify grant writing. There is a certain way to do it, a certain way things should be written and presented. There is also the foundation's cost-benefit ratio—for how much they are going to give you for your project, who and how many benefit. Know what you're doing here so you don't waste other people's time and waste your own in the process. And the last and most important point to remember with foundation money is that if your topic is the slightest bit controversial or if the filmmakers could possibly jeopardize the status and stature of that particular foundation, you can pretty much forget even being in the running for a grant.

The second major effort in fund-raising was trying to reach individuals and small production companies that might have an interest in our subject matter or, with my sappy long-form synopsis, to snag a soft heart. Brian gave me a book, the *Hollywood Creative Directory*, that lists every major production company, studio, and producing entity, and I went through and highlighted all people and entities that had anything to do with documentaries or children's feature films or TV shows. I started a personal letter-writing campaign to try to secure either funds or participation.

I received some pretty amazing responses, but no money. While I wasn't surprised, I was not defeated either. People are very personal with their money. Even the richest of the rich don't just give their money away without thinking about it. However, I knew that I needed only one person who cared about arts in education or maybe loved ballroom dancing to throw in the first $10K or lend their famous name, if that was the case, and then I could get the ball rolling. Many of these people sent not form letters but personal notes of encouragement. These notes came from a whole host of Hollywood and industry people—quite an impressive list—and because I was quite flattered, it helped keep me motivated. There was a lot of genuine "rooting" for the project. I found that people who knew the moviemaking business genuinely cheered on anyone trying to make one. It's too difficult an endeavor not to be supportive of those attempting this crazy feat independently.

The third approach was a letter-writing campaign to corporations that supported arts in education or anything closely related. I was much more focused here because corporations follow philanthropic guidelines. It was very similar to applying for grants. Corporations' Web sites outline their causes and application processes and this helps narrow the field of reach. My major focus was Target Corporation, whose complete philanthropic focus *is* arts in education on a local and national level. I thought they'd be a perfect fit and, besides, I had this little idea—another dream—that if we could partner with Target, maybe, just maybe, we could get Target to develop a merchandising campaign to match the movie and generate more revenues to dedicate to arts programs in every state. I was trying to work all angles but nothing ever came of it.

A couple things happened, some very funny, that moved the project forward, and in a way solidified the fact that we had something and should be a little less eager to give it away. Besides general support and appreciation for the idea, we got interest not in the documentary but in the rights to a fictional movie version instead. We also got inquiries about television rights. Of course, it dawned on me that this concept could be "sliced and diced," franchised into a lot of different products, going in a lot of different directions. My mind started thinking about all the possibilities. I had already thought of merchandising but now I started to think of every possible broadcast creation all the way to an animated series on a children's network. Think *The Cosby Kids* ballroom dancing. This caused me to take a break from fund-raising and jump into action to write a fiction film treatment from the not-yet-made documentary. I copyrighted every document I wrote that had anything to do with the doc—including the sales kit components. I started to gather information on trademarks.

As these tell-tale signs began coming to the surface, and I kept working to create, record, and protect all aspects of the franchise, we slowly began to shut out anyone who had contacted us, deciding eventually it was better to fly under the radar. I remember telling Marilyn that we were on to something and that if we made the movie well, we might really, well . . . have something.

But as we were coming up on the end-of-year holidays, we had chosen our schools and researched equipment and crew, but didn't have a cent. We decided we would just have to do what most first-time filmmakers do—self-finance. This was not an easy decision. It actually wasn't even a decision, so it was *just not easy*. This is the one area where I had to really ignore the fact that money has any value and think of it as just a tool. A tool to be used to get something else. Something more valuable. I had to believe this to be true, and I did.

ACTION PLAN

1. Write a letter to your friends and family that will either let them off the hook or let you off the hook later on.

2. Create a sales kit. Include the business plan, articles about your subject and/or documentary success stories, the budget, and anything else that will help sell your idea. Don't overload the kit with too much information. People are busy. Don't overimpress. In the end, it will be your passion and drive that convince others that not only is it a good idea but that you also have the energy and commitment to see the job through—from beginning to end.

3. Research Web sites for your target fund-raising audience. This will include nonprofits and corporations. Start making a target list.

4. If your topic is academic in nature or socially relevant, investigate hiring a grant writer. Or take a course in grant writing, do your own reading and research about grant writing, or find a good friend who is a grant writer and write some grants.

5. Target individuals and production companies and/or in-house development executives in the media (at networks, cable stations, and so on) where you will find your desired audience. Use the latest edition of the *Hollywood Creative Directory* as a guide.

6. Seek out support or funding from corporations but don't jeopardize the integrity of your film with product placement or other types of corporate promotions. Merchandising after the fact may be possible—if it's all for a good cause. Just don't mix, or even blend, the art of documentary filmmaking with anything other than telling your story.

7. Come up with your marketing "slice-o-matic" list. If the idea does appear to be a franchise, make a list of every way the idea might be marketable—remake, television series, stage, music, merchandising, retail stores, and so on. The franchising aspect of the project will add value. It will be a more attractive package for potential buyers, hopefully, later on.

8. Be prepared to spend a little bit of money on the fund-raising research end, as it will help you save money down the line by knowing exactly who the target audience is in seeking these funds.

9. If you don't get any money, don't give up. You can always mortgage your house (*Hustle & Flow*), do it on credit cards (*Spellbound*), or borrow from the bank . . . or relatives. According to the finance book I read, 95 percent of first-time docs are self-financed. In this case, remember that, with making art, money is just a tool with which to make that art. However, know that this *is* very tough to do.

5

Copyright and Clearances

THE MUSIC

*W*hile there were several things to look into possibly clearing, such as archival footage, photographs, artwork, and exposed product names or titles, the main copyright and clearing function on *Mad Hot Ballroom* was music.

The first thing I did was a get a list from ABrT of all the music they play in the classroom. It included about thirty songs total. I made a chart listing each song and then I started to search the music databases—the American Society of Composers, Authors and Publishers (ASCAP); Broadcast Music, Inc. (BMI); and the Society of European Stage Authors and Composers (SESAC)—to find the publishers attached to each song to obtain the publishing licenses (better known as synch licenses). From a friend, I borrowed two directories, the Pollstar Record Company Roster and the A&R Registry, that list all the record companies to obtain information about clearing for the master use licenses. There would be clearing costs involved and I wanted to get an idea of what this type of project, with the music we wanted, would entail.

When I started getting some rough quotes back, I realized there was a problem. We would never be able to get this project off the ground with the kind of fees that were being quoted. The music costs would be prohibitive to any documentary filmmaker who thinks this story would make a good subject, because the music is embedded in the story and must be used. But I felt that there had to be a way, and it really came down to tenaciously begging, and accepting that our music budget would be much more than we had anticipated. It was quite a challenge. Those who make music clearing their livelihood really deserve kudos if they are getting it done efficiently, without having to throw down an antacid tablet every four hours.

We ended up hiring a music supervisor to help me with this grueling process. The toughest songs to clear were "Hit the Road Jack" by Buster Poindexter (which we ended up not getting because it was owned by Ray Charles and he was very protective of the overuse of it), "Fever" by Peggy Lee, "Gonna Make You Sweat" by C + C Music Factory, and "You're Driving Me Crazy" by Della Reese. In code, these songs, flying back and forth in e-mails, were Hit, Fever, Sweat, Crazy. That pretty much sums up the experience for me.

With music, bite the bullet and find the money to hire the experts and companies who do this for a living. Music clearing is not for the fainthearted. Research films that have soundtracks you like and find the music supervisor in the credits. Go from there. You may not need a music supervisor but you will need a clearing person or company, as this is the "nuts and bolts" to getting the music you want. However, hiring a great music supervisor takes all this off your plate. If you do hire a music supervisor, make sure this person is capable from the start. It's important to make sure he or she takes the job all the way through contracts, because that, too, is a job unto itself. This is another area, in addition to fund-raising, where you really get to ask only once.

Asking once means taking the time to figure out the music budget ahead of time. With *Mad Hot Ballroom*, our music budget was originally $80K. When all the final bills came in, it had more than doubled. Most films' music budgets fall between 1 percent and 10 percent of the total budget. If you have big, big songs, add another 10 percent to 15 percent on top of this, especially for a small-budget film. In the end, our music budget represented 40 percent of our total budget. As a documentarian, don't be unrealistic. You can have twenty fairly unknown songs or one U2 song. You choose.

Read a book about music clearing so you can talk intelligently with your music clearer or supervisor. Know the difference between synch licenses (the published words and music) and master licenses (the record company owns it with a particular singer singing the song). Know the music clearing terminology (usage, media, territory, term, most favored nation, same use, and so on). There are all kinds of music request forms and license samples in books specializing in copyright and clearances.

In the beginning, you can clear the music just for festival use, which gives you permission to show the movie with your chosen music only at film festivals, to help save on your budget. If there is an interest in your film, then run back, quickly, and clear all your music commercially and get ready to pay, since this is the filmmaker's responsibility and not paid for by the studio. We tried to get as many as possible of these commercial quotes in writing when we were requesting festival licensing so that we could adjust our budget accordingly and know what we would be getting ourselves into *and* we could hold a music entity to a specific quote if suddenly the doc sold. If the music publishers or record companies know a big studio is attached to the project or is about to be attached, and you don't have the quotes in writing, you can basically kiss that music budget good-bye. Your choice might then be replacing the music with lesser-known songs that you might not like. This may be all right in the long run if the music is just dropped into the soundtrack of the film. If the music is source material (meaning recorded when you are filming, so it's on the film itself and was not added in later as was the case with *Mad Hot Ballroom*), it will get very expensive further along in the edit to replace it.

If going it alone, be strong and keep on top of your requests. There is a big pile on the music executive's desk, and your doc song request for $1,000 doesn't hold a candle to Applebee's requesting the same song, where the music company will make $500,000. Hunker down and keep calling them. It pays to be persistent.

There are many creative options. You have to look for them. You can find your own composers and have the songs and score originally composed and orchestrated. You then have to clear only publishing rights and you can have the song sung by your neighbor who has a great voice, and the recording studio will cost you one tenth of what the master recording license will cost you, if even that.

When filming, watch out for background music in stores, cars, bars, and everywhere else. If it can be identified, it has to be cleared. We filmed and thus recorded a cell phone tune when Rosie, the mother of Michael, the young boy from Bensonhurst, answers her phone while walking down the street. It was classic because it was six seconds of the tune "Gonna Fly Now," the theme song from the movie *Rocky*. That wonderful six-second moment that said so much *and* gave a good laugh cost us $2,500, and this was after weeks and weeks of talking the publishing company down from $10,000. However, note that fair use laws are coming on strong and by the time you make your documentary, you *might* be able to film freely without worry (but don't hold your breath).

Overall, do not mess around with the music industry. There are a lot of filmmaker/music horror stories out there. Do not go to a festival without clearing for festival use. It will come back to bite you. It has for others and the teeth marks will be on your wallet.

RELEASES

*W*ith *Mad Hot Ballroom*, we had more than seven hundred release forms (legally written permission forms to film a subject) from start to finish. Even though some of the people never made it into the final cut, we were covered. We also had a special form, which was not much different from the short form, for minors.

Every time you interview a person for your doc, get a signed release. No ifs, ands, or buts . . . do it. Don't think for a minute that you will go back at rough-cut stage and get the releases. You won't. You will be buried in other stuff and that guy you interviewed on the corner is no longer on the corner. But you can bet he'll see the movie somewhere and if not happy with his portrayal, he might sue. Why take any chances?

You will need a production lawyer and he or she will write the necessary language for the release form. Or you can look on the Internet to see if there are some samples that you can then tailor to your project's needs or, best bet yet, ask a filmmaker friend or anyone in production for a sample release form. But make sure that when you actually use the release form you've had your production lawyer review and approve it.

LOCATIONS

*W*hen filming, permission is needed for almost all commercial locations. Get a location release form signed for every location. You'd be surprised how this one seemingly simple thing can get filmmakers into a bind later on. It's not sexy but it's necessary. Building owners and managers will treat this matter as the most serious, most important thing in the world.

We had our own interesting challenge with regard to location and it wasn't pretty. We had gotten permission from the New York City Department of Education (DOE) to film the program in the schools back in October 2003. I received approval communicating that it was up to the principals of each particular school and as long as they supervised it, we were fine. On one of the scouting trips, the principal of a school we visited in the Bronx said she'd seen a new regulation about having to get special permission to film in the schools during school hours. It didn't really register because we had already gotten permission. On the same day, we went to scout P.S. 112 in Bensonhurst (this school ended up in the movie) and again the principal brought up the new regulation and mentioned that we should look into it. There was a new communications director at the DOE, and this new regulation was just put into writing— that only news crews or nonprofit entities were allowed to film inside schools during school hours. We were neither.

My heart skipped a beat but I thought that our prior approval would hold. We went back to confirm our permission only to find that the Communications Office had changed their minds two weeks before filming. Changing the dance classes to after school was not an option because all the kids had other afterschool commitments. We couldn't get ABrT to change their schedules. It was logistically impossible with more than forty teachers' schedules, the kids' schedules, and each school's facility availability. In a state of shock, Marilyn and I proceeded to call and e-mail everyone we knew who knew anyone at the DOE.

Those days were excruciatingly painful because it was the first time the project had hit a wall where it would be decided whether we could continue or not. I thought it was crazy that we were suddenly at an abrupt stop—something I'm most definitely not used to. I remember I had a little stand-up gig in the Village and, though I pulled it off, I was a basket case. Marilyn and Brian were there. We all went out to dinner afterward. Brian and Charlie started telling me and Marilyn that we should work what was happening with the DOE into the story. Marilyn was quiet. She would wait. She has an innate ability, whether learned or genetic, I don't know, to wait things out. But while calm on the outside, she was completely stressed about it too. We were both worried it would be the end right then and there. All I know is that I remember telling Brian and Charlie, "I can't be Michael Moore," referring to taking on the DOE in an adversarial way. "That would be very stressful! I just want to make a charming story about kids ballroom dancing!" And we all cracked up.

After many phone calls, sleepless nights, and other endless worries, I received a call from Chancellor Joel Klein's assistant. We got permission to film in our chosen public schools during school hours three days before we were set to start filming. We hadn't said anything to our crew because we didn't want to look like fools. It was a tense period, but we were determined.

It's important to remember permits to film are needed for almost everything and especially every location—parks, buildings, streets, in front of buildings, bridges, and all forms of public transportation, almost everywhere. This is where the local film and television commission comes into play and where you apply for permits to do the filming. Brian showed me the ropes with all these aspects. While a somewhat simple task, it takes up some time and the detail requirement is on the heavy side, so plan for it.

OTHER CLEARING ISSUES

We met with a copyright and clearance lawyer just to go over what you can and cannot do with documentaries. For example, you can't alter reality—no moving a picture or moving furniture. This is interesting, as it raises certain questions: What if there is a known work of art behind a person, and you know that to clear usage of having that artwork in the picture would be totally cost prohibitive? What do you do? Move the person? It gets tricky.

Learn about E&O (errors and omissions) insurance and how much this will cover you legally with all that you film. An insurance company views the film and then you get coverage to compensate for any possible damage that might be caused by either negligent mistakes or unknown infringement. It's expensive but worth it. It should cover you from here to Timbuktu because in today's litigious society, you never know what might happen.

Know the fair use laws. They are currently being challenged to hopefully benefit the documentary filmmaker more, but know them anyway. *Only you* can make sure you've crossed all your *t*'s and dotted all your *i*'s.

And last, with regard to copyrights and trademarks, as I mentioned earlier, we did copyright every piece of writing tied to the documentary. Once we came up with the name, which you cannot copyright, I trademarked it. The title *Mad Hot Ballroom* and *Mad Hot* was filed every which way. So if they ever want to do merchandising on the remake, and come out with Mad Hot perfume or a Mad Hot Ballroom dance line, the trademark names belong to us.

Make sure you have a great production lawyer who either knows all this or has good connections with other lawyers who specialize in these areas (music, fair use, and copyright/trademark). The bottom line is . . . protect your product and protect yourself.

ACTION PLAN

1. Hire a music supervisor or work with a major music clearing house.

2. Figure out your music budget ahead of time and keep adjusting it so that you know where you stand and where the music stands in your budget at all times.

3. Read a book about copyrights and clearing. Know the lingo.

4. Clear just for festivals to help save on your budget. Get commercial quotes in writing early. A distributor will expect the filmmaker to cover all music expenses. It's a bummer but they do not pick up the tab for this.

5. If you're up to the challenge or under extreme budgetary constraints and you do take on the music alone, be strong and keep on top of your requests. Make sure you have a good therapist or friend to whom you can vent.

6. There are always many creative music options. Look for them. It's a big country, a big world, for that matter, and there is a breakout singer and musician in every other basement, garage, or rooftop waiting for a chance to be heard.

7. Be a hawk about all kinds of sounds everywhere making their way onto your footage. If a subject even hums or just says the words to a song but with enough of a rhythm to recognize the tune, it will have to be cleared. Remember these wonderful words: if it can be identified, clear it.

8. Interview a person? Get a release. These days I'd even get a release from the owner of a dog that happens to cut across your frame.

9. Know your fair use laws (www.centerforsocialmedia.org/fairuse.htm).

10. Get a location release form signed for all locations.

11. Get a copy of an E&O (errors and omissions) insurance application and learn what it is all about and how much it costs. This will serve to protect you after your film is done, mostly from possible frivolous lawsuits.

12. Copyright (www.copyright.gov) and trademark (www. uspto.gov) everything you can think of. Copyright all writing tied to the documentary (outline, synopsis, treatment, pitch letter) and trademark the movie title under Entertainment Services (you cannot copyright a movie title). And while trademarking the title, trademark any other realistic derivative of the name in case there are future merchandising opportunities.

13. Hire a production lawyer way in advance.

6

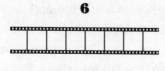

Scouting

*T*o get to the core of your idea, you must first dig the hole and then try to build a fence around it. This is done through research. It's intensive research, on this project, or any project, that helps define the parameters. I had done the proper research on the subject and now Marilyn and I set out to research the boundaries of what we'd be filming. This is called scouting.

We took all my research and, based on the outline of the story at that time, we scouted not only the subjects and potential subjects, but also the locations—schools, parks, and neighborhoods in general. We did this very early on, in the fall, and it was great to break up the monotony of fund-raising. It helps to look for what will seem to work, what might look right, and what obstacles might pop up with any of these people, places, or things. However, it's important to keep in mind that scouting is a continuous process in documentary filmmaking. Unlike a narrative film for which every shoot has to be scheduled and official with permits, documentary locations can be scouted and the paperwork filed for only what you know at the time. As we started to film our documentary, things came up and we found ourselves scurrying to the permit office to add a park or entering a building or restaurant at a moment's notice that required a location release to be signed on the spot.

While scouting seems like a fun and easy thing to do, it is really the beginning of digging the hole you are about to jump into. How big and how deep is completely up to you. And the things that come up that fall into that hole, on top of or alongside you, are all yours for the duration of project! It is these elements that make the filmmaking journey quite unpredictable and challenging . . . and certainly worth it. It's good to get an idea, early on, of what is in store.

THE SCHOOLS

We got a list of all the participating schools from American Ballroom Theater. That particular year, the 2003/2004 school year, there were sixty schools. They were in every borough (Manhattan, Brooklyn, the Bronx, Queens, and Staten Island) but there were only a few schools in Staten Island and those schools did not compete in the competitions. We had another meeting with Yvonne and Pierre to talk about some of the schools they thought might make good subjects.

We scouted twenty schools that were certain to compete in the program. We originally envisioned choosing four schools— one from each borough. We researched many factors: the teachers, the teaching artists from ABrT, the facilities, the neighborhoods, the logistics of filming (light, sound, location), the time slots, and the overall gut feeling about the school and its "personality."

We narrowed it down to five schools. Since we had only

one school in Brooklyn, P.S. 112, that one stayed and, fair enough, it fit our criteria nicely. The schools in the Bronx were very nice and the children were lovely, but there was not a distinct enough characteristic or "personality" with either Bronx school. They were not that different from the Brooklyn school. If we were going to have an uptown school, the schools in Harlem and Washington Heights fit many more of our dimensions and had a more vibrant feel.

I had always wanted to go back to the 2003 winners (to see what they were up to), so P.S. 144 would represent Queens. While I was writing the article, even though P.S. 150 in TriBeCa did not make it past the semifinals in 2003, I went to the final competition to check out "what might have been." It was there that I saw P.S. 144 take the big trophy and I was very impressed with their confident style. I knew if one of our other three chosen schools made it to the finals, they'd most likely be going up against P.S. 144 again and it would be great to play the two schools off each other. There was also a very strong point in the original outline where one of the big burning questions that came to my mind was "Who were last year's winners and what are they up to this year?" Questions like these, when writing your initial synopsis or outline, help you define and flush out your story.

I stayed fixated on following P.S. 150, the school in TriBeCa from my original article. This is a unique city public school because, as I mentioned before, there is only one class per grade. These kids had been together since kindergarten, so they were more intimate with one another, but also insular. While smart and streetwise, these kids were a little more protected. They were cushioned a little more by privileged economics, nurtured by professional parents, and affected by the proper but sometimes stifling etiquette of political correctness. But this also made these kids stand out. TriBeCa's P.S. 150 eliminated the opportunity to follow P.S. 11 in Chelsea, which was also on our scout list, because the ABrT teaching artist Alex Tchassov taught at both schools. So we cinched P.S. 150, TriBeCa, and Alex. Alex brought a new flavor to the pot, as he is an immigrant from Russia. He had been a very well-known dancer in Moscow, where he had his own television show. He gave up a lot to come to America but told us that he came for basically one reason—to make money to support his family. All the acclaim in Russia didn't pay the bills, let alone help him get ahead.

The key to choosing the Bensonhurst school, P.S. 112, was Victoria Malvagno, the ABrT teaching artist who taught there (as she says in the movie: "The people upstairs are sleeping. Downstairs the party's going on"). She has a magnified presence, and we thought she would be a good person to help move the story along with regard to the details about the dance instruction. As an added benefit, the neighborhood thrilled us with its transitional spirit. In the past five years, the previously almost all Italian neighborhood had become more than 50 percent Asian. The challenge was that there were three classes and we had time to follow only one—and there was one that felt just right. A little boy with some great facial expressions, Michael, swayed us, and we ended up lucking out in the end because three of the six dance team couples were chosen from this particular class, so those kids were familiar to the audience until the end (which was a good thing, as we ended up having so many kids in the film for the audience to try to remember).

The last decision, and the hardest, was deciding between the upper Manhattan schools in Washington Heights and Harlem. We chose P.S. 115 in Washington Heights because of teacher Yomaira Reynoso. She is strong, interesting, and confident. We felt she was going to give us "a story" because of her dynamo nature, which rocked us from day one. Also, ABrT teaching artist Rodney Lopez complemented Yomaira's verve with a lovely touch of class. The school had a certain inner-city charm to it—a little rough, which showed character, but not too ghettoized. It was still an elementary school so there wasn't the kind of wear and tear on the school, the teachers, and the kids that you'd find in some tough high schools. And that was fine by us. We never wanted the grit to take away from the objective of our real story.

Once we decided that these were the three schools we would follow and film, I monitored their classes for the rest of the fall semester. Two or three times a week I'd drive to the schools and take notes on the class structure, the personalities, the dynamics of the kids with the teacher and with one another—even though they were not the kids we'd be following. I felt it was a way to get the lay of the land before we went in to film. I wanted the teachers and school administrators to get to know me and feel comfortable with what we would soon be doing. A couple of times while I was monitoring the three schools, I would get extremely paranoid that maybe there wasn't a story—that I was chasing some kind of false creative notion. This happened once at P.S. 144 when I had brought a couple of potential investors out there to "see" how cool it was, and it wasn't—*that* day. That time at P.S. 144 was the closest I had ever come to having an anxiety attack about the film, and so I fought the feeling and soldiered on. The thought that it wasn't a story was a monkey on my back and I had to consciously disengage my fears. I was able to do this because of one simple thought, which has everything to do with being a mother: If it wasn't something having to do with my kids or husband, their health and well-being, it wasn't anything to fear. It's that simple. My own family is the great "leap in life" barometer.

Despite my anxieties, another benefit to monitoring the fall semester classes at these schools was that I started to get a feel for each neighborhood. The neighborhoods became characters. I drove around a lot before and after classes to get a sense of each street, the local stores and shops . . . the overall essence. I became excited to share these observations with Marilyn, who was dealing with her family happenings and also working (as she was about to take a major pay cut by doing this documentary). And she got it. She also saw all these things about the city. It was the weird and wonderful neighborhood characteristics that she loved about the city too.

I think the biggest obstacle with any of my creative discoveries was my own enthusiasm for what I saw and heard. How would we take all these fun and funny things and make sure they got onto film? How would we take something we saw and make it translate to the story in the movie? How would we get it right? Marilyn and I talked and laughed about these ironies all the time, much to the dismay of our families and friends, who eventually had to tell us they had heard it all before, way too many times. I think many thought we were crazy.

Even in my own neighborhood I saw the strange and lovely. I saw TriBeCa kids going to school in a building where large food trucks pull up and unload food, the kids having to maneuver around the hand trucks and boxes; business executives harried from their commutes negotiating the crowded and chaotic streets, with the kids in the neighborhood going to school by all modes and means; and cars pulling into parking lots and getting loaded onto racks and maneuvered up into the air, four high, to make room for yet more cars.

In Bensonhurst, every house had a lawn decorated as if in competition. Whether religious statues or the current holiday decorations, the tchotchkes were maxed out. And every day around noon, everyone who was home came out to wait for the mailman. Each house seemed to have something that made it unique, as if the owner had to make a statement in his or her own way. Add to that the fact that several ethnic groups were now mixed into a neighborhood that was once all Italian. It certainly added a whole range of flavor to the house and lawn decor extravaganza.

In Washington Heights, the produce sold on the street was different than in my neighborhood—what *were* those big purple vegetables? While there was a Dominican flag hanging on almost every traffic light, there was also an American flag right next to it, and BUSH FOR PRESIDENT signs in all the storefront windows, in one of the poorest neighborhoods in Manhattan. Street vendors sold everything from summer ice drinks to ladies' lingerie.

All three neighborhoods had a major bridge that defined them and was indicative of the soul of the streets. These majestic structures that brought the rest of the world into this great city were positioned in each neighborhood as if on lookout. I remember exactly the day I said to the crew, "We should have the bridges in the film—representing each neighborhood" as I was staring right down the street at the silvery, glistening bridge in Washington Heights. Not only did those bridges represent each neighborhood, to everyone everywhere else, these bridges represented New York City.

Washington Heights had the George Washington Bridge. This huge, looming steel structure rising up above the neighborhood represented movement and a path to another place. I thought the bridge was significant for this group of people, mostly Dominican immigrants.

The Verrazano Bridge came to grandly hold court over Bensonhurst, and that it led from Brooklyn to Staten Island seemed fitting—"Who needed to go farther than that?"

The Brooklyn Bridge regally gave TriBeCa an entrance. Old and majestic and stately, it represented a group of kids who would know that the Brooklyn Bridge had a rich and complicated history behind it—similar to the karma of many of those kids.

The subway system is also a character. Marilyn had thought we might be able to use it graphically in the film to "move" the story from place to place. It plays a major role in many New Yorkers' daily lives. The giant transportation system is as simple as the colors of the subway lines. The numbers in the colored circles displayed at each entrance and exit say so much about every daily journey of more than eight million people. Life in New York City makes it easy to take these markers for granted when they really become part of one's daily blueprint of existence. For example, I'm a red line gal. I like the other subway lines but I'm never hesitant to jump on the 1, 2, or 3 to get where I'm going. The other lines, the yellow, green, blue—and other colors that I'd have to look at a map to use!—don't speak to me. I'm all red line. Ask other New Yorkers and you will see, they are what they ride.

It was this knack for seeing the strange and the wacky and the wonderful that made me see how rich this city is and how much it has to say without ever having to say anything at all. The visuals were there and they were great. My perspective was from the outside looking in—as if everything were foreign. Having spent my formative years in the Midwest fostered this, and being a writer certainly helped. And Marilyn, having been raised here, loves New York City and everything about it. She always said that *Mad Hot Ballroom* is her love poem to New York.

ACTION PLAN

1. Get to the core of your idea through the initial subject research (Chapter 3) and then scout to map out just where you are headed. This helps define the parameters.

2. The writer sets the tone of the project. In our case, the writer and director drove the project. Not all documentaries will claim a writer but I think they should. The writer of any documentary is the one who conceptualizes the idea on paper to take it to the next level. If the writer and director are one and the same, it's a bonus for getting it right. I have read and heard that some of the best writers are also directors and vice versa.

3. Get out there and see, feel, taste, hear, smell, sense, investigate, devour—everything. This is your blank canvas. Gather the colors onto your palette that you'll eventually use to paint your picture.

4. On your scouts, organize which location (streets, bridges, schools, and so on) filming permits you'll need to secure in advance (in New York these are filed and applied for at the Mayor's Office of Film, Theatre and Broadcasting). Be ready and have the infrastructure to do this spontaneously if need be once you start filming.

5. Along with your regular release forms for people, make sure you have an ample supply of location release forms too—every day. Get these release forms signed (both

personal and location) ahead of shooting once you have narrowed down your chosen subjects. Second best would be securing them right before a shoot. Least best, get them on the spot the day of the shoot. But get them.

6. This is where the advice "plan ahead" is emphasized.

7

The Business Side of Things

It was fun planning to make the movie. The whole business side of things was another story. Similar to fund-raising, it's not enjoyable unless you make it so. That's not easy. There is a lot to consider. It definitely can bog you down but what other choice is there? As with physical exercise, just do it and get it done. Set things up effectively and efficiently and stay on top of them. Think beyond the business box and it will become more fun. In the meantime, get a shot of espresso before reading this chapter.

THE LAWYER

Things tend to pop up in the world of filmmaking, even if you are "just a mom making a little movie about dancing kids." The list is long and the obstacles great but, as our lawyer told us, the more successful the movie, the greater the chance of lawsuits. Whether it's someone saying they had the same idea, or subjects feeling they didn't get anything out of it, or a location stating they never gave permission to film on the premises, every filmmaker has a story. As a filmmaker, you do the best you can to protect yourself and do all your paperwork diligently. The old saying that you never want to have a lawyer until you need one is true. And what is even truer is that once you need one, you need a good one. So we didn't slough off in this area.

We secured a lawyer early on—four months before filming began. Besides protection, there are numerous other reasons we needed a production lawyer *ahead* of time to help chart our course. We got the lowdown on what can and cannot be done, what we needed to do, and what we needed to avoid, and we had someone watching our steps and watching our backs. When the questions "Can we do this?" or "What's this mean?" came up, it meant we needed to ask our lawyer. And yes, with all the lawyer jokes out there, it's like admitting you watch reality TV to admit you have a lawyer, but that's the way the world goes round.

How do you find a good lawyer? Ask around and get referrals. Talk to other filmmakers and interview at least six lawyers. We did this and then we followed our guts and employed the one with whom we felt most comfortable. Make sure of one thing—your lawyer must think like you do. Don't employ the nice "we can all work this out" guy if you are a fighter. Hire a fighter. If you like to keep it all nice and peaceful, then by all means find a lawyer who works it all out in a peaceful way. If you do not find a legal kindred spirit, you will be fighting and/or negotiating with your own lawyer all the time—and that is what he or she needs to be doing for you with others.

Decide up front how you are going to pay your lawyer. It should be a percentage of the sale of the film or a flat hourly rate. Some lawyers will ask for a credit too (associate producer, for example). There are advantages and disadvantages to both the percentage and the hourly rate. If you can gauge your legal load and the value of your movie fairly well, this choice is easier. Because we were new to all the particulars of the legal aspects of filmmaking, we opted for a percentage because we knew there would be a lot of discussions. If you have done this before, know a lot about it, and can streamline the legal process, go hourly.

The irony is that I, someone who had never really had a lawyer, had seven lawyers surrounding me by the time the whole *Mad Hot Ballroom* trip slowed to a walk: three for the movie, two for stage, one for the foundation I created (with a focus on arts in education), and a personal lawyer for my new work. But no litigators yet, and I hope we won't ever need one (no offense to litigators).

THE BUDGET

*B*udgeting is kind of fascinating. It's probably good to think of it this way: It's interesting to see toward what and where your money goes and how close you come to estimating expenses correctly. So before we could set out to find any money, we made a budget. The budget started out small and just grew and grew along with our project. Marilyn did our budget on an Association of Independent Commercial Producers (AICP) budget application. This was sufficient for us. From what I've heard, the way to go is Movie Magic, touted as great budgeting software for moviemakers. Regardless, the AICP program served our purpose—and I'm sure no budgeting program is a deterrent to rising costs.

You can try to control some cost areas throughout the process. After coming up with a basic cost for just the actual production of a typical shoot day, which would include the cameraperson's and soundperson's day rate, meals, production supplies such as lighting and film stock, and transportation costs, we then multiplied this amount by the number of days we scheduled to shoot the doc. These are the variable costs, meaning they increase or decrease with the number of days you shoot. This gave us a very firm pure production cost. Some other costs are based on a percentage of the variable costs or total estimated budget. For example, a music budget is usually between 1 percent and 10 percent of a large film budget and can be up to 25 percent of a smaller indie film or doc budget. You pull all the possible estimated costs together, including fixed costs such as insurance, equipment, legal and accounting fees, and above-the-line salaries, and record them into a report. A book about budgets helped me through this process of making sense of what things would cost, as it offered estimates for all the production functions, but I basically relied on Marilyn's knowledge, and Brian's too, since he had provided her with his expertise in this area.

The thing that made *Mad Hot Ballroom* more expensive than many other documentaries from the get-go was that we were going to shoot for four months consecutively. We were not raising money and shooting and then doing the same again later on down the road. When it was to be up and running, we would be up and running and there would never be the option to go back. These particular kids danced that one season, for that one competition, and we were following them. The event was a finite experience and would never happen again the same way. This is why Marilyn wanted to start the editing function earlier than usual. We were going to have to shoot a lot of video in order to get what we would want to make the movie. While we planned every shoot day and tried to plan each one with particular shots, many times it was as if we were winging it, which is a huge part of documentary filmmaking. We spent a lot of time just following those kids around, trying to capture their journey leading up to the competitions.

Marilyn came in with the first budget, and it was basic. It would've paid for the director of photography (DP, also called the cinematographer), if even that, and the blank videotape stock. We were just starting to feel this out, to throw some numbers down. Somehow that budget became just something to laugh at and then the next one increased to $120,000. This was more like it, but still bare bones.

As I read more about production, and Marilyn and I discussed it, to really attract the right talent, pay ourselves, and do it the right way, we'd have to increase the budget. So Marilyn did another budget and came back at $240,000. The higher the budget got, the more I realized this was for real.

As I mentioned earlier, the last thing I wanted to do was approach possible fund-raising entities with one number and then come back to them with a larger number later on. We had to go in with one number and stick with it.

I said to Marilyn, "That's fine, let's keep the one working budget of $240,000, but give me a 'blue-sky' budget—if we could have it all, what that number would be." She came back with a budget of $450,000, and at that moment, we knew, that's what it was going to cost. This would be just what it was going to cost us to make it with a very low number for music rights. We didn't include transferring to film and all that entailed or the postproduction supervisory expenses. We didn't know our music budget was going to more than double. I can now report that the final cost—with everything included—came in at $725,000.

(Similar to real estate construction, it reminds me of the saying "Twice as much and twice as long.")

We had a fairly good blueprint to follow. I was amazed that Marilyn plugged in the numbers with a flair for getting her estimates within pennies of the actual numbers. She was exemplary with the details of our budget and there is security in following financial budgeting guidelines, since it helped us make decisions and set up parameters within which to work.

THE BUSINESS ENTITY

There are a couple of ways you can set up the business entity for making a film. You can use your own money, but this is obviously problematic if you don't have any. You can borrow money from relatives and own the whole thing outright—with intentions of paying people back over time. This can be nerve-racking.

There are a couple of other alternatives. You can obtain a loan from a bank, which is fairly straightforward. However, you have to have collateral.

You can seek a fiscal sponsor. A fiscal sponsor is a nonprofit organization—a 501(c)3—that has arranged to take on projects and endeavors that may use their nonprofit status in exchange for a fee charged by the nonprofit. Of course, the mother ship nonprofit entity has to follow certain rules of what type of projects they can take on according to what their focus is, but in most cases, you can find fiscal sponsors either in your chosen film subject area (most documentaries are set up under fiscal sponsors because of the social and/or cultural aspects) or offered by organizations within the film industry (say, Women In Film, to name one).

Unless you have someone who is ready to make a huge donation to you for your film and wants the charitable write-off, I'd hold off on establishing your business entity until you know where your money is coming from. The charitable fiscal sponsorship was not going to work for us since we had no foundations with grants or corporations with donations and therefore we didn't need the nonprofit status. Nor did we want to pay the 5 to 7 percent fee on our own or with bank-borrowed money if that's what it came down to. As of this writing, there are new hybrid filmmaking business setups that are one part limited liability company (LLC) and another part nonprofit under a fiscal sponsor.

We didn't decide on our entity until after five months of futile fund-raising, grant writing, and begging—and this was one month before shooting. Since we hadn't any money, we decided it was best to incorporate and try to sell shares to potential investors. I investigated the different types of incorporation and the LLC seemed to fit. After finding out how much lawyers can charge for incorporation services, I did it myself at midnight, online, for $200—directly with the state of New York government.

The LLC is a good option if you think you really might have a marketable film or at least one that will break even. It provides all the same benefits of the other business entities, and more. You have greater control. You provide your investors with approximately the same write-off opportunity as a nonprofit does. No one takes a fee (except the lawyer and accountant and then, relative to the nonprofit fee, it might come out a wash). The biggest benefit is that if your revenues exceed your costs, the profits go to the filmmakers and the investors (how much to whom depends on how you set up your LLC). Another huge plus is that an LLC protects you and your own pockets in the case of lawsuits. You will eventually need an accountant and a lawyer, even if you set it up yourself.

Search the Internet and you'll find your state government Web site and instructions on how to incorporate. You can also do name searches on the site (as well as on the USPTO—United States Patent and Trademark Office—site) to see if the name you want is taken by a company that has incorporated nationally (interstate). Filmmakers usually have fairly creative production company names, so it's rare that you will find another entity out there with the same name, but sometimes it can happen.

And, of course, this reminds me that the most important thing Marilyn and I had to decide up front was what the name was going to be. This is one of the highlights of setting up shop—naming the company! One night, Marilyn and I were discussing everything we had to do and we ordered a glass of wine. The waitress came by and asked us if we wanted another round. Since we've been known to go down this path before many, many times and haven't stopped at one, I jokingly said, "Marilyn, if we are going to get this movie made, I think I need to stop at *just one*." She laughed and agreed.

The name was confirmed a couple weeks later when I was telling her about the challenges of the music choices that Pierre, Yvonne, and I had originally narrowed down to about thirty songs. I had done initial research on the costs of these songs and it was going to be extremely prohibitive. I was especially fixated on the Peggy Lee song "Fever," which was played so much the year before when I wrote the article and continued to be played in the monitored classrooms that fall that I knew it had to be in the selection. Marilyn mentioned that we could use lesser-known, not-as-popular music and I turned to her and said, "I want all the original music. If I'm going to make *just one* movie in my life, it has to be perfect."

So JustOne Productions it became. Once Marilyn and I were having a meeting and we got a call from a telemarketer who asked for what sounded like "Just Stoned" Productions. We laughed. It fit.

ACTION PLAN

1. Get a lawyer early on. Get referrals. Interview a half dozen or so. Then follow your gut and go with the one you think you can work with the longest and who most respects and reflects *your* style.

2. Decide up front how you are going to pay your lawyer. It should be a percentage or a flat hourly rate. Some lawyers will ask for a credit too (associate producer, for example).

3. From here on in, and forever more, starting with the contract with your lawyer (once you find one), read every one of your contracts. Read every word. Read those contracts as if they were material that you will be asked on a game show where the prize is a million bucks and you *have* to win. It's easy to throw these down and then say later you "kind of" read them. It's best to take the time to really do it.

4. Before you set out to find the money, make a budget. I've listed a great budget book in Appendix B.

5. Financial options for making a film:

   - Use your own money.

   - Borrow money from relatives and friends and own the whole thing outright—with intentions of paying people back over time.

   - Take out a loan from a bank.

   - Seek a fiscal sponsor, if seeking nonprofit status.

   - Form an LLC and sell membership interests.

6. If you form an LLC, search the Internet to find the state government Web site and the instructions on how to organize the entity.

7. Have fun finding a name for your production company. Remember you have to live with it a long time. Too cute gets stupid and not cute enough gets lost.

8. Get an accountant who knows the movie business.

8

Getting Started: Crew, Equipment, and Logistics

GETTING STARTED

$\mathcal{I}$t was early 2004 and we were ready to hire crew. Marilyn, with help from Brian, who had a list of any and all crew possibilities, focused on this function since she had worked in the industry for years and knew who to talk to based on what we were looking for. She started by looking for a DP and checking their reels, which are examples of their work. She narrowed it down to two, and then she shared their work with me. I viewed the reels and I listened to her explain what she liked about each and who might be more fitting for this job. As a layman at this, but with an artist's eye, all I could do was just look at clips and then think about how they moved me. I relied only on intuition as that was all that I had with regard to this practice. I certainly trusted Marilyn's eye and knowledge for this process.

With actual production just around the corner, we were gearing up both physically and, more important, mentally. Everything was set to unfold. I was nervous, excited, and frankly too busy to let any of these feelings cripple me. The funny thing about production, or certainly about documentary filmmaking, is that it is very similar to a runner's high, that feeling you get when running long distances. It's about the anticipation of going on this journey, not knowing where it will lead. The idea of spending a large amount of money on something unknown was dangerously exciting. Most exciting to me, from a creative standpoint, was that I was putting everything and anything I had ever done in my life, a culmination of all my experiences, skills, and talents, behind this one project. I was going for the gold . . . the big trophy.

THE CREW

*M*arilyn often says she leaned toward Claudia Raschke-Robinson for our DP because of the work on her reel. Marilyn told me she responded to Claudia's reel because of the intimacy of her shooting as a storyteller. She thought Claudia's work had that very sensitive feel that would be very good filming children. There were several documentaries on the reel, and in particular one called *I Am Beautiful* that had caught Marilyn's eye. Marilyn first met with Claudia alone, and they talked endlessly and easily about the cinematic visions Marilyn had for the film. Marilyn and Claudia discussed many films, including *Unmade Beds*, because it contained portraits of the city. Marilyn wanted to use portraits of the city and wanted these scenes to play out with the bigger picture. Claudia understood and after this initial meeting it was quite clear that Claudia had the right sensibility and feeling.

So she was the right fit for the project, but would the project fit her? This was a difficult project schedule-wise. Most DPs are used to working for a chunk of time, but we were asking whoever came on board to work two or three days a week for four months. It would be hard for Claudia to have to tell other producers and directors that came along that she was available only on Tuesdays and Thursdays. We would be asking the DP to give up a lot in the way of possible missed work opportunities. Claudia was aware of this work aspect, but loved the project, and the greatest thing was that she wasn't going to let other people shoot in her place; she wanted to "own" it—which of course was very good for us.

Claudia was a joy to work with; I always say she is sunshine in human form. When I first met her, she was friendly and polite. It was not until we began working together that I found this wonderful contrast of take-charge attitude mixed with high-energy optimism that made me watch her in awe. She had a hearty laugh, but more than that she embraced life and everything about it and that came through in everything she did. She also really got into taking filmmaking to another level—the psychological level. We had a kind of hyper-chemistry in this department—we could take a subject and, in intense discussion, break it down to its psychological, sociological, physiological, and economic components. Claudia added to the already established bond between Marilyn and me. She complemented us.

There was never a doubt in Marilyn's mind that she wanted to bring on Sabine Krayenbühl as editor. Marilyn had been following Sabine's career in fiction and documentary films for a long time, and they had worked together years ago. Sabine has amazing storytelling skills, and Marilyn knew she would be a great collaborator and would help to shape this film from the beginning. Marilyn had been courting Sabine for a while. She had told Sabine that she wanted to talk to her about editing this documentary film. One night she and her husband came to Marilyn and Brian's house for the weekend. After dinner, Marilyn said to Sabine, "What's on your schedule for the next six months to a year?" She replied, half joking, but half serious too, "Your project. What is it?"

Sabine became excited over the same things we did but did so from in front of the screen. Adding Sabine's enthusiasm to the group brought the project to a level of shared consciousness that was quite magical at the time. Only now, in hindsight, can we see this to its fullest degree, but we knew we had something. We were all on the same page, in the same head. But Sabine added one more thing to the mix. She is extremely sharp and has a genius way of turning something around. She often saw something from a completely different angle, picked up on something that no one else had seen, and was able to pull this out as a crucial element in the storytelling process. She would offer up something and the rest of us would say, "That's incredible!" We also liked the way that, when we'd go to visit her in the editing room to drop off some more tapes, it was as if she were on a delayed timer. We would be one week ahead in shooting and she'd say something about one of the kids from the last week's shoot, such as "Where's Amber? I noticed she's not in the shots as much." And we would have to fill her in on why there was less of Amber, or another kid of whom Sabine had grown fond on her screen earlier, who wasn't in a later set of tapes. All our thoughts became consumed with the characters on the screen: they became a part of our daily lives.

Once the DP and editor were in place, we needed a sound person. Marilyn had a list of good sound mixers and it really came down to availability and economics. Marilyn said our project was tricky because of the possibly tiny voices of the kids and the large role the music would play, literally and figuratively. We needed a good sound person with a lot of experience. Marilyn spoke to Brian about this and he suggested Tammy Douglas, who then joined the team.

Marilyn, Claudia, Tammy, and I made up the estrogen-packed, liberal, NewYork–opinionated, globally diverse, divergently partnered, politically passionate, and passionately political crew. We shared four months in a beat-up, old, dirty vehicle making a film about kids ballroom dancing. We always said, "What is said in the van, stays in the van." We had a great group dynamic and it was just easy to be together—and that ease continued throughout the project. Moods were announced first thing in the morning: "I'm happy," "I'm tired," "I had a fight with my husband and I'm feeling vulnerable," "I'm quiet," and compassion was offered if it was wanted or attitude adjustments were made throughout the day to accommodate those in certain moods. We developed a special team-oriented relationship—like a group of younger women on a traveling sports team, except that we were "just a little bit" older women in a minivan.

THE EQUIPMENT

The next thing we did was buy the camera, the tripod, the monitor, and some other peripheral equipment (see the list at the end of the chapter). As a beginning filmmaker, I had absolutely no experience with equipment. This was a whole different ball game. If I hadn't had Marilyn's experience in this area and had wanted to get going on a project and needed equipment, I would have found others in the industry, other directors, and particularly DPs, and asked them what they use to shoot, which cameras they like and dislike, and why. I would have also looked at films I liked and then looked someone up on the credits to find out what they used, and bought the same equipment. Obviously this would be a first-time filmmaker's approach. (There is a copy of our equipment list and what everything cost at the end of the chapter.)

Marilyn and Claudia thoroughly researched it and thought out every detail, the overall essence and purpose of the film, and decided what camera would be best. Our ballroom dancing documentary by its nature, with regard to the many hours of coverage, required a camera package that delivered rich images at an affordable cost. We chose the twenty-four-frame (24p) digital video format. It closely mimics the look of film in both texture and substance. It was the right choice for our subject matter— children, dancing, and their contrasting environments—and for this complex and intricately woven story. The camera also had to be small in size to be unobtrusive, almost hidden, which it eventually seemed like it was—in Claudia's belly. With the flip-out feature on the Panasonic AG-DVX 100A 24p camera, Claudia was able to hold it at her waist to shoot at the level of the kids, which invited the audience to be at their "level," and their age, during the movie.

The cinematography encompassed natural light (mostly because we didn't have a lot of money in our budget for lighting) and utilized the camera as a fluid, moving partner in the storytelling, as Marilyn had envisioned. Claudia used close-ups and portraits to gain a feeling of intimacy and insight, as she was known to do and do very well.

The contrasting movement of dance and the close-ups of beautiful cityscapes—culturally representative, "as-if painted" silhouettes—conveyed the surprising, subtle differences between the three geographical locations of the featured schools and their diverse, colorful populations. This seemed to really say, in a nutshell, what Marilyn and I, with her keen eye and love for New York City and my voyeuristic obsession with the city, had talked about capturing all the time. The style was intimate and vérité, with little static photography. The 24p, in actuality, offered a soft and supple force both in focus and composition.

It was always our intention and hope that this documentary would be transferred to 35mm film. Every decision made with regard to shooting had been developed with that in mind. This camera would prove to handle the transfer effortlessly, as it matched frame per frame (24p), rather than regular video, which shoots thirty frames per second.

I loved our camera but we also had a fairly big problem of the sound dropping out. That footage is gold! To have scenes ruined because of this one "little" sound glitch made our hearts skip a beat or two. It ended up just being a loose screw, which happens often to this model and make, but it was something we didn't catch until it was too late. So check your equipment all the time and have it serviced during or in between shoots.

THE LOGISTICS

In the beginning, we collected footage as if casting a giant net to see what we could pull in. We used a production schedule, calendar, and daily shot list (see the end of the chapter) and we juggled the information on these three documents to obtain rhyme and reason for what we were catching in our net.

We planned every shoot. We thought about the who, what, when, where, and how of every possible aspect of the film and then put it through the "What do I need? Why do I need it? And how do I get it?" questions. We discussed everything all the time and when Marilyn and I were not together (which was rare), we kept thinking about everything all the time. This is why the original outline is so important. We took that outline and turned it into a shooting schedule based on what we were looking for. Then we took that shooting schedule and bundled all similar geography or subject matter into same-day shots. The shooting may have been out of sequence from the outline but we got the footage nonetheless. A DP and sound person work a full day (ten to twelve hours, depending on what's contracted). Use them a full day or time and money are wasted. Since we were shooting in a finite period of time, we used the changing of the seasons to help show the passing of time in the movie. We didn't have to worry about the continuity problems other documentarians shooting over a longer period of, say, many years might worry about. It's wise to go over what those issues might be and keep an eye open for seasons changing, daily weather changes, or kids growing! While some of these issues are not as important as shooting out of sequence on a fiction film, it is still something to think about.

Once we planned out our shooting schedule, we broke down each day into a list of every possible shot we wanted. We utilized the full day by adding on b-roll shots—landscape, ambient, or cultural shots, or anything that adds, surrounds, supports, or emphasizes a-roll shots, which are the shots of the subjects, basically the spine of our story.

We worked all this into a production calendar. We may have started with a rough draft of the four-month shoot but basically we went month to month and even then, it was updated weekly. Subject availability, schedules, new things that pop up, all contribute to the daily changing of the production schedule. We charted out what we knew we couldn't do, thus allowing us to know what we could do and when.

For example, we knew we could only interview the kids at home after school or on weekends but obviously never at school. We knew we were tied into ABrT's dance lesson schedule. Shots were often neighborhood driven. If we were in Bensonhurst one day, we'd schedule the whole day there with shooting the dance class, and then neighborhood shots, and then going home with one of the kids after school. With documentaries, you end up with a lot of footage you don't use. So fill up those days and hope for the best. If you find yourself in situations where it's just not working out, continue filming and soldier on. It's all a process.

Before every shoot day we made up a shot list. Marilyn and I would either do it in the car at the end of a day or we'd e-mail each other, each adding to the other's list. We'd also update the questions, if need be, to adjust to the direction in which the film was going.

Marilyn brought Sabine on early because *Mad Hot Ballroom* was a story that would unfold during our production. Sabine and Marilyn discussed the footage after each shooting day, and Sabine assembled little scenes right from the beginning. This was great because they could see what was working well, watch the development of different characters, and experiment with different ways of cutting the classroom scenes to compress time. Marilyn told Sabine what themes we were looking out for and which characters stood out, and Sabine told Marilyn which scenes were working very well and, in some cases, to shoot different things that she needed. During the shooting, in addition to building scenes, Sabine was also building bins of footage divided by school, character, dance, and so on. We also created bins filled with clips of quotes from the kids. These bins had labels such as LIVING IN NEW YORK, BOYS AND GIRLS, WHAT I WANT TO BE WHEN I GROW UP, BEING A KID, WASHINGTON HEIGHTS. The intention was to build montages of quotes, and interrupt the narrative with these montages.

This kind of collaboration was really valuable because we were not going to get a second chance for pick-up shots. We were on a one-way time line. There was no going back.

This was a magical experience and one of the reasons that docs are so cool. You start off going after one thread in a story, and the film editor steps in to direct you to the thread you are meant to catch. Sabine was key in that she had a trained eye and a creative mind, so she was able to see these threads come up and know they'd be worth pursuing. The process between Marilyn and Sabine was a dream come true to us, as we were so far into the forest when shooting, it was sometimes hard to see the trees. Having this continuous massive flow of collection, dissemination, evaluation, and then direction of content, as if the story were in fluid motion, helps tremendously in seeing where you need to go on a daily basis when shooting.

ACTION PLAN

1. Recruit and build your filmmaking team. Your budget will determine who and how many will be in the crew, and in what roles, from producer and director all the way to production assistants.

2. As much as hiring is a big part of the job, firing is sometimes a reality too. Remember this if you are

working with friends. Define your roles and always secure and sign legitimate labor contracts (called deal memos in the industry).

3. For those of you interested in our equipment list and in how much "hard assets" cost us then, here's the list:

MAD HOT EQUIPMENT LIST (2004 prices)

PANASONIC AG-DVX 100A 24P MINI DV CAMCORDER	3449.95
CENTURY PRECISION .7X WIDE ANGLE CONVERTER LENS	649.95
CHROSZIEL 4X4 SUNSHADE W/ FRENCH FLAG	799.95
PANASONIC CGAD54 9-HR LITH BATTERY PACK	169.00
POWER-2000 CHARGER (2)	79.90
PELICAN #1600 EQUIPMENT CASE W/FOAM INSERT	114.95
JVC TM-91OSU 9" PROF COLOR MONITOR	594.95
TIFFEN 4X4 POLARIZER FILTER	128.95
COMPREHENSIVE S-VIDEO CABLE	21.99
PORTA-BRACE MO-900 FIELD MONITOR HOLDER	199.95
VINTEN PRO-6DCV SYSTEM TRIPOD	1150.00
TOTAL:	**7359.54**

4. If you have a director and DP, they are instrumental in making the equipment choices. If you are doing this on your own, get opinions about equipment from as many directors and DPs as possible.

5. Check your equipment all the time and have it serviced during or in between shoots.

6. Plan your shoot. Think about the who, what, when, where, and how of every possible aspect of the film and then ask the relevant questions.

7. Create a production calendar. While our final calendar is printed here, it did not start out like this. Start with a rough draft and update it as needed.

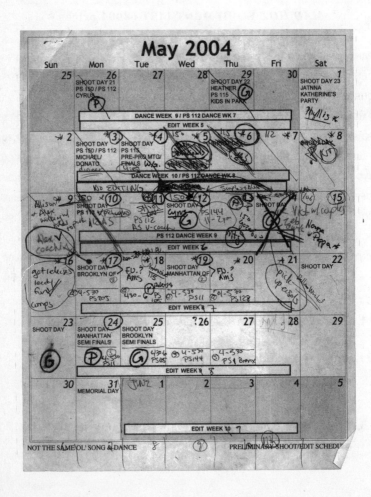

8. Create a production schedule based on your calendar and bundle similar shots based on geography or subject matter. These will then be selected out by week and used on a weekly basis to keep you on track.

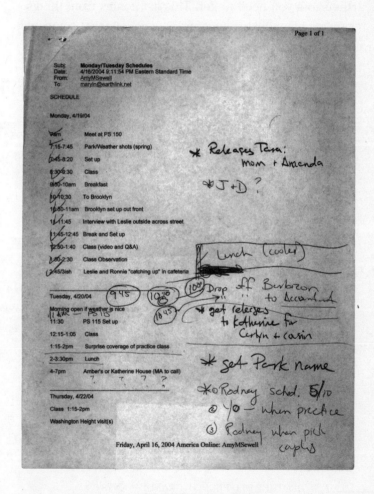

9. Take the production schedule and break down every day into a list of every possible shot you want to get; this is called the shot list. Add in b-roll shots.

10. If you have the editor on board early, get his or her comments on a daily basis.

11. Then build what we called a "Shot Wish List," listing all the shots you need to get. This list comes from things you are planning to shoot and suggestions that come up later from daily discussions and from the editor's comments, and everyone else in the crew who comes up with bright ideas along the way. The collaboration at this time, with ideas flying around and thoughts coming to the surface, truly makes the actual production both stimulating and exhilarating.

We categorized by school and then by "character," added exterior shots on the end, and shot these as filler on days we had the time. Use something that is easy to read and that can be updated easily, as you will be doing it often.

A typical shot list for *Mad Hot Ballroom* looked like the following (this has been shortened to one tenth of the original document and shows only one school):

THINGS TO SHOOT AS OF MAY 26

P.S. 112

MICHAEL—

- SOCIAL EVENT WITH FAMILY & DANCING
- POEM / ESSAY ABOUT DANCING

BENJAMIN—

- W/ BROTHER/OLD PEOPLE (GRANDPARENTS?)
  AT NEIGHBORHOOD PARK

EXT. SCHOOL—

- KIDS AT RECESS **—

KIDS—

- LETTERS, ESSAYS FROM KIDS—

NEIGHBORHOOD—

- SURROUNDING NEIGHBORHOOD WITH AN ASIAN FEEL
- COLLECTION OF CRAZY "WELCOME TO BROOKLYN" SIGNS
- SUBWAY PLATFORM / SIGN

9

Getting the Footage:
The Neighborhoods Set the Stage

*T*he importance of the next three chapters, which cover the actual filming, or getting the footage, as I've referred to it, is to understand that the basic idea *is* that you are working on creating something, hopefully something wonderful, and what is that going to take? What will it involve? Who and what will take up that space? What will it turn out to be? How will you get it there?

Thinking as a painter, I thought about how I approach my art. How large will the canvas be? What colors will make up the palate? What brushes will be used? Broad strokes or small, supple, mastered strokes? Thick application? Thin and watered down? Style: Abstract? Expressionistic? Realist? Surreal? It's a good way to relate to how a filmmaker goes about deciding what actually to capture when he or she starts gathering footage and to the particulars of how exactly this is done. While it's easy to read books or listen to teachers and professors tell you what needs to be done, it's rare to actually hear how it's done—task by task but encompassing the bigger picture too—so that it'll be that much easier to see it, to actually feel it, and to get out and do it. It's more interesting if told as a story. This was ours:

The first week of the program we decided to film every day to get us up and running, and in the frame of mind of what to expect. P.S. 112, in Bensonhurst, was not starting their program for another couple of weeks, so we started our full week diving into P.S. 115 in Washington Heights and P.S. 150 in TriBeCa, and we spent one day at P.S. 144, the previous year's winning school in Queens, just to get a lay of all the lands.

There were to be ten weeks of actual dance lessons in which the kids learn, in this order, the merengue, the foxtrot, the rumba, the tango, and swing. There were other dances too, such as the polka, the waltz, and some line dances, but we focused on these five main dances because those were the dances in which the kids would eventually compete. With a couple more weeks of intensive training and then the weeks of the competitions, we filmed a total of about four and a half months straight.

Every morning the crew would meet outside my apartment. I'd bring down the camera gear and we'd pile into my old white minivan. We either picked up the lighting the night before a shoot or we had it for the week. In the beginning, the most important thing was getting into a shooting rhythm. We were going to be in this a long time, and on a schedule, and there is something to be said for finding that working pace and incorporating, like an orchestra, everyone's personal rhythms.

The first week of filming involved two things: the introduction to many of our major "characters"—the teachers, the principals, the ABrT dance teachers, and the schools—and the development of a pattern, building stamina for the long haul in front of us. When you stack up the basic components of our movie—the city and its traffic; school rules and the principals who follow them by the book; the parents of the kids, who, while mostly very nice and accommodating, still gave us the "you mess with my kid and I'll ..." look; and the kids themselves—we had our work cut out for us.

At P.S. 150, we met Alex, the ABrT teacher, and Allison Sheniak, the schoolteacher. Alex was a lovely, soft-spoken man. His Russian accent made everything he said sound melodious. We were very fond of him. He was nervous from the start about the kids taking the competition too seriously. Allison worried about us filming her kids, and like a mother lion, she guarded her cubs.

Pierre, the codirector of ABrT, was introduced, as it was his custom to start off the first class in the program in each school. He began the introduction like a movie star, exaggerating his voice and his moves with dramatic appeal. The kids really liked him because he made them laugh.

At P.S. 115, we met the teacher, Yomaira Reynoso, and also Rodney Lopez, the ABrT teaching artist. Yomaira's spunk was unprecedented. She had a bring-it-on attitude every day. Her youthful looks and small stature made her blend right in with her kids but when she spoke, you knew she was the teacher. Rodney was a gentleman from the start. He exuded a quiet disposition but a strong core. His intimate sense of groove made him likable to everyone. They were a twosome we couldn't help but watch all the time.

We met the whole gang from P.S. 144 in Queens. We filmed their culminating dance show and got a good idea of what it was going to be like filming the competitions to come—chaotic! It was good to establish ourselves in Queens so that we could fly back in there later on without a hitch.

Our shots were the basics: getting used to the dance areas; the first dance, which was the merengue; the teachers and kids coming and going from the schools; and the neighborhoods. We threw ourselves right in and started interviewing the adults, including the principals, to have them explain the start of the program, talk about their kids, and talk about their history—to hear their stories and what made them interesting.

Besides the weeks of the competitions, this was the only week we filmed five days. From then on, it was only two or three days of filming a week, with several weekends thrown in along the way, when the kids started to feel comfortable enough with us to spend a day here and there with them at home.

Very early on, it was all about the program and the way the teacher taught the classes. After a couple weeks of hearing the instruction and filming the classes, I realized that we had too many days scheduled to shoot the classes. Marilyn had been worried about that from the start and voiced her concerns but I didn't want to cut down on the days. I remember my biggest fear was that we would miss something. I think this is common when shooting a doc. It was hard to remember that we couldn't get it all and we wouldn't get it all. However, this fear will propel efficiency, to try to get as much as possible. It did make us reevaluate how we were going to spend our shoot days.

We ended up looking to get more footage of the daily lives of those in the story. We started thinking about filming before and after school and taking some of the kids out of class, two and three at a time, to talk to them about this process they were experiencing. We also continued to interview the teachers, principals, and dance teachers. It was interesting to gauge how they felt starting out and how they would feel through the progression. It was also a great way to get them used to us and familiar with our setup and procedures. At this point, we had a great group of people. We were very respectful of each school and the rules. This is where the small, all-woman crew, the small camera, and the minimal lighting, if any, really made us unobtrusive and amenable to our surroundings.

It was in filming the kids, the way they started to open up to us, that Marilyn came up with an idea that would take this story and move it to another plane. One of the first nights during production after we had finished shooting for a day, about 10 p.m., we were walking down to my corner deli to get something to eat for dinner. It had been a long day and we both had our heads down, quietly discussing the kids we had worked with that day. There was a moment of silence and then Marilyn stopped, turned to me, and said, "Amy, I want this story to be told from the kids' perspectives. I want everyone to be at their level, in their world." And as she said this, she had her hands up to her face, holding an imaginary camera, and she took it and swooped it down to her belly. And this fit with how Claudia had been shooting since the beginning. With a camera that usually was held at eye level, Claudia, using the viewfinder flipped open and out, shot from belly level. It was at this point that it had now moved over to become a movie about kids growing up in New York City and the dancing just became the thread that held it together.

THE NEIGHBORHOODS BECOME CHARACTERS

Washington Heights

*E*ach neighborhood had its own character and within these neighborhoods there were challenges. Washington Heights was exciting. This is a poor but vibrant neighborhood, close to the George Washington Bridge, which, unfortunately, makes it a major drug selling depot, as it is the gateway from the more well-to-do suburbs in New Jersey. People from the suburbs can get in and buy their drugs and get back out to sell them to other better-off buyers.

It is a tough neighborhood but there is a strong cultural foundation and emphasis on family. Fathers and mothers work, many times more than one job. If they are not there to raise their kids because they are working, a relative or friend watches the kids. Marilyn was touched and reminded of her father when she saw three elderly men on the corner. Many times we would see a grandfather walking a grandchild or grandchildren to school. It was a beautiful picture. These were some of the hardest-working people I've ever met and protecting their kids was a priority. There was more love and warmth up there on those streets than I had ever witnessed in my life.

It also had its scary quirks. One day on a shoot, Marilyn and the crew found themselves in the middle of a police raid. I wasn't there, but I heard about it! They were interviewing Yomaira, with her kids, in the middle of a fairly nice Washington Heights restaurant. There was a group of big guys behind them at a table. Marilyn asked them if it was okay to film, they'd be in the background, you know, no big deal, no focus on them. They agreed. Within minutes, the cop cars came flying up and cops came rushing in with guns drawn, followed by the whole "everyone down on the floor" *Top Cops* maneuver. With their heads on the floor, Yomaira on top of her kids, Claudia whispered in Marilyn's ear, "You want me to keep filming, right?" and Marilyn, with her face squashed to the floor, nodded yes. Claudia kept rolling. A couple of the guys were arrested. Once the restaurant was cleared of the suspects, the interview continued—kids and all.

Another day, I ran to get my minivan and said hello to some big guys sprawled out in lounge chairs on the street. I started pulling out my keys to get in my car, and one guy jumped up and went for something by my tire. I jumped a little but thought, Oh, he must be moving a bottle from my tire path so I won't get a flat tire! I thanked him. He looked stunned.

I said, "Didn't you just remove a bottle from my tire path?"

He said, "Huh?"

I stumbled, walked back by the back tire, and started feeling my pockets; I thought maybe I had dropped my cell phone or wad of petty cash.

I said, "Did I drop something?"

These big, geared-up guys wearing logo'd clothes were just staring at me like I had landed from another planet. I looked down at the tire well and saw the tailpipe of my van. And then I got it. They were dealers using my van's tailpipe as a storage unit while they worked the corner close to where I parked.

Ohhhhhhh!, I thought, feeling ridiculous. I smiled, winked, got in my car, and drove off. The whole crew had a laugh over the adventure. I really was much more concerned about the crew's safety. I couldn't just put them in situations where someone might end up hurt. We never saw those guys again, but there were always other guys out there on the streets and I took note to get our filming done, be polite, and get the crew home safely.

There came a time when we also felt the streets protecting us in a strange sort of way. Once word had spread that we were making a good movie about the neighborhood kids, the vibe on the street changed. We were welcomed, larger than life, with hugs and cries of "Hola, mami!" in Washington Heights. The smaller the living space, the bigger the hearts. What a gift to have had the chance to immerse ourselves and be welcomed with such open arms and big hearts.

We had never experienced more love and care among family members (even if the parents were strict), and it all seems to make so much sense now, looking back, that all this feeling would directly correlate to how those kids dance. When they couldn't speak it, they showed it. When they had nothing, they had nothing to lose. There weren't any barriers, especially on the dance floor, and this came through loud and clear.

TriBeCa

TriBeCa was a little harder for me to "see" because I live there, but having twins who were five years old at the time helped a lot. They had started kindergarten at the other local TriBeCa public school (not the one in the movie), and I had started looking at their surroundings when I was writing the article when they were in first grade. By the time I had started research on the doc, my daily walks to school with them became fodder for the continued research efforts. It was always about looking to see how different their world, at this age, was from my world at that age—especially as city kids.

My kids navigated busy streets and handled incoming spontaneous noise (fire trucks, honking, yelling, subway rumblings from below, and so on) without flinching. They went to school where large trucks loaded and unloaded a variety of things. They dealt with businesspeople in a rush, bicycle messengers whizzing by the wrong way on a one-way street, the subways, the taxis, the garbage trucks, and people—lots of them, angry at the day, frustrated by the obstacles, manic type-As conquering the city as beast, those just trying to get by, and those who got lost along the way and were planted right outside the building, yelling at the demons in their world or just plain looking for money for food, drink, or drugs.

To my kids, this was their norm. They were also TriBeCa kids, and as I got to know the other kids, in Washington Heights and in Bensonhurst, I could start to see what my own kids took for granted at such a young age. I could see a certain level of emotional and psychological entitlement, both in the physical realm of what is tangible, but even more so in the intangible realm of what is yet to come—or should I say, expected to come. My antennae were up more in TriBeCa just because these daily patterns, daily happenings, and daily circumstances were harder to see since I lived them too, but they started to show themselves—quite vividly.

We started to notice Town Cars taking kids to school; parents, running late, who have the option of taking their kids to school in taxis; the fantastic outfits on the moms—who look good even if they're wearing their own type of morning sweats; the fact there are a lot of dads at or around the school (meaning they can afford the time with their kids; they work in creative fields, and had achieved a level where they could have this time, or are big-time professionals whose time and how they use it is never questioned); and the accessories of the kids: scooters, shoes with wheels, iPods, coats and hats and gloves that are cool and interesting—one of a kind—a privileged set's fashion show. Flowers are sold in TriBeCa. I don't remember seeing flowers sold in Washington Heights. Flowers for the sake of flowers are a luxury. Chefs and the kitchen staff of the finest five-star restaurants gather outside daily and eat their own food. There are large dogs because there are large apartments. Dog owners can afford to employ dog walkers and pay more to have their dog walked with only one other dog or alone, so the dog receives individual attention. And individual attention, whether for dogs, kids, or adults in TriBeCa, is the keystone to the neighborhood. It is a neighborhood where the drive, or demand, for individual attention is a collective unconscious consciousness.

It's a neighborhood in its own state of constant transformation, from artist pioneers in the sixties and seventies, to the ever-constant push toward the astronomically unaffordable, and still the hot place to be, hang out, work, and live. TriBeCa, like a Sesame Street, is a little enclave surrounded by the big city, and it has a feel of being safe. One of our biggest challenges was to find enough contrasting influences and color in TriBeCa to equal what we saw in Washington Heights. We had to get beyond TriBeCa's "beige," as it seemed under the glaring glow of Washington Heights' "red."

There were visuals that were indicative of the neighborhood and added to its presentation in the film. The streets were clean and bright. The building architecture was historically maintained. Storefront windows had meticulous and elegant displays. Because the buildings are not tall, there is not overcrowding, and you could walk anywhere without having to maneuver as if you were in a video game, as you do on the Upper West Side, where every venture out on the street is like a human obstacle course. The people walking around wore interesting outfits, hip glasses, and great shoes. And the ones who didn't were probably our resident movie stars (and film directors!).

Bensonhurst, Brooklyn

Bensonhurst was another fun neighborhood to discover. There were not many people out and about, unless it was time for the mail to be delivered. Then everyone came out on their porches and waited for the mailman as he came down the street. We discovered this one day as we were filming, and thought the neighbors were doing a *West Side Story* thing by coming out, arms crossed, to kind of size us up and demand an answer to what we were doing with a big black camera in front of their houses. It took us a couple minutes to realize that they were just waiting for the mailman! That this June Cleaver scenario, in this day and age, is part of the core of one of the biggest and most demanding cities in the world, threw me off. It's a great way to describe Bensonhurst in Brooklyn. Kids had good sneakers and dressed in normal kids' gear, T-shirts and blue jeans. This was the quintessential little blue-collar neighborhood. This once 100 percent Italian neighborhood had become more than 50 percent Asian over the previous five years. There were still Italian restaurants and delis—one that touted having THE best mozzarella in the world. On almost every front lawn of the Italian households, exactly three feet by five feet and sometimes fenced in from the sidewalk, were at least two statues, of Mary and Jesus, of course! St. Anthony occasionally graced us with his presence every other house or two.

Forest Hills, Queens

The school neighborhood of Forest Hills, Queens, gave us another angle. It could have been anywhere in the United States, but it was about eleven miles away from Manhattan. The streets were clean, and so very different, so suburban, and the lawns small and well manicured. The houses were expensive because of their location. The school was a nice facility, quiet and well run. The dance class was multicultural and totally diverse. The teachers cared . . . a lot. The parents were involved. The kids were not only smart but had many talents as well. What else could anyone ask for? They were the perfect school in the perfect neighborhood and everything always seemed right.

We had numerous shots that didn't make it into the movie, but used enough to show that TriBeCa exuded a temperate aura; Washington Heights, an electrifying flavor; Brooklyn, the safe feeling from a bygone time; and Queens, a refuge, away from the hustle of the city, but attached at the hip to the giant machine no less. The neighborhoods started to define New York City for what it really is—an amazing melting pot where eleven million people co-exist, with all their bells and whistles, within a geographical area of 20 square miles.

Our canvas was big and our palette was full.

ACTION PLAN

1. Lighting. Hmmmm. It is as good a time as any to bring up lighting. We had very minimal lighting. It was really bare bones. I personally like shooting with natural light. Ever since I read that the revered documentarian D. A. Pennebaker doesn't care for lighting either, I don't feel so embarrassed to admit it. I didn't like having to depend on lighting to get the shot. I felt it was a hindrance. It is also costly. But that is just me. After this project and two feet into the next doc right now, I can still tell you that I prefer shooting with natural light. However, Marilyn, and especially Claudia, as it is one of the pillars of her profession, were well versed in lighting needs and requirements. You need lighting for many things, in many instances, and many times, so as a beginner, make sure you are working with someone who recognizes the requirements for the lighting function. Your DP will know and you can trust that the DP will want to get the most beautiful shot ever and so the lighting equipment list will never be sparse. In fact, it helps to know enough about lighting to be able to cut

your DP's lighting list suggestions in half or you will blow your budget.

2. Be creative with the options of shooting the landscape. We shot out of the minivan sunroof to film the neighborhoods. We made our car into a dolly (usually a cart and track that holds the cameraperson moves along at the side of the subject to get the shot in motion). With a light touch on the gas pedal to keep at a constant five miles per hour and cars beeping behind us or people yelling, "You idiots!" at us from passing cars, Claudia and the camera beamed out of the sunroof to catch these shots.

3. Get to the top of certain buildings to get aerial shots of the neighborhoods. You don't need a crane for these shots. You just need to be able to sweet-talk building lobby entrance security guards.

4. Look around you. See beyond what is there. Look at "your picture." This is the backdrop of your movie and it can be fantastic.

10

Character Development:
The "Cast" of Characters Emerges

*I*f the neighborhoods are the backdrops, the characters are the colors. And how bright and vibrant they were. While a documentary doesn't always allow for such choice of subjects, with our film we were lucky in that so many shone so brilliantly. The fact that the subjects were kids also helped.

THE STARS AMONG US

*I*t was obvious that when we filmed the kids, and then watched the dailies, the cast of characters began to emerge. The kids we thought might pop out didn't. And those we didn't even notice during class suddenly showed up, right there in front of us on film, as if they had some sort of unspoken communication with the camera.

GRABBING YOUR HEART:
THE STARS OF
WASHINGTON HEIGHTS

The very first day we walked in to scout P.S. 115 in Washington Heights, we met Yomaira. Small in stature but powerful in stance, wearing a putty-colored warm-up suit with a whistle around her neck, she put her hands on her hips and demanded, "Well . . . are you going to make me a star?"

Well . . . , I thought, taken aback. "It's just a little idea, a little doc, a very small movie. We hope it will even be a movie," I mumbled. Yomaira seemed not to hear. The principal, Ms. Zeppie, peered out her office door and Yomaira yelled to her, "Ms. Zeppie, they're going to make me a star!"

"I knew your day would come," Ms. Zeppie enthusiastically replied.

This made me nervous. It was a lesson about keeping expectations to a minimum (including my own). Yomaira did, however, no surprise, add a great deal to the film.

There was no "glossing over" with Ms. Zeppie, and that is why we had one of the best interviews with her. Whether she spoke about the kids ("What's going to happen to them? Are they going to be successful in junior high school or not? Are they going to succumb to the temptations out there or not? You know, you want to . . . almost . . . be their protectors. And you can't.") or the neighborhood ("It's a very challenging place. The streets are not clean. Everything happens outside. Very little happens inside. Washington Heights does not sleep. Life is in the streets.") or the people ("People are trying to make a living. They're trying to keep their heads above water. They do whatever it is they need to do to survive."), there was no beating around the bush with Ms. Zeppie. She was direct and honest and this was favored by the camera. When subjects are themselves, they come off very well. When subjects pose or act, trying to be something or someone they're not, they ring false and it comes off as embarrassing.

We got lucky with many of the adults because they were solid enough and brave enough to be themselves on camera. The luxury of filming kids, especially at this age of eleven years, is that they can't help but be themselves. Those little kids, all of whom didn't say a word the first couple of weeks, slowly, like peeling an onion, one layer at a time, eventually started to give us more and more and more. The first little boy who ruffled our composure was the boy who is referred to at every film festival, every Q&A (question and answer session) around the world as "the boy with those eyes"—Wilson. Claudia had a hard time pulling the camera away from him and going to other kids. And you could see it on the dailies too. He really came through. And it wasn't just women who loved this kid. Wilson hit everyone's radar.

Marilyn and I both knew during filming that there was more behind each kid than we chose to put in. That poverty breeds crime is an old story. That kids from divorced or broken homes have a tougher time in the long run is not a surprise. We wanted to make a movie about hope. In addition, we felt a personal responsibility because the parents entrusted us with their kids. I felt as if I had more of this weight on my shoulders when we were filming in my neighborhood and, since I have kids myself, I knew what that meant. But Marilyn felt it just as strongly, especially in Washington Heights, where she had really identified with the kids. This was a huge psychological burden. We had great responsibility.

At Wilson's house we filmed Wilson and his sidekick, Danilo, doing their homework on the couch, eating a candy or two. I remember we asked them about the other kids but as with all kids this age, they didn't feel comfortable talking about other kids. They felt it was wrong to "talk behind another's back." It was in this scene that Danilo asked Wilson who he thought was cute and Wilson replied, "The girl with the long, dark hair." That was a description that fit all of the girls, so it was funny.

Wilson and Danilo grew attached to the crew. They always seemed to be around when we were filming not only the class but also other things around the school and outside. They were curious in nature but they also kind of got to be *our* sidekicks. They asked a lot of questions about how, what, and why we were doing what we were doing. Of course they'd ask these questions in Spanish and Marilyn would always have to answer them in Spanish. Wilson ended up calling Marilyn *maestra*, which means *teacher*.

Two little girls caught our hearts in the beginning, too, Rafaela and Scarlyn. They were actually the two who gave me the idea for the name of our movie. I had been knocking around a name involving a two- or three-word title, knowing that *ballroom* had to be the last word. The first part of the title had to be either a two-syllable word or two words. For about two months a lot of suggestions were flying around the minivan. Then one day, we were filming Rafaela and Scarlyn walking down the street and Rafaela mentioned that she liked to move her hips.

"It's mad hot," she said.

It's a great little scene where she goes on talking about dancing with a boy. It's one of my favorite scenes. It was those two words, *mad hot*, that made me investigate in all the other neighborhoods if this was global or only unique to Washington Heights. Once I discovered that all ten- and eleven-year-olds placed *mad*, which means *very*, in front of anything—mad hot, mad cool, mad paranoid, mad crazy—I knew we had the title of our movie, *Mad Hot Ballroom*. After polling the crew in the van one morning, it was accepted unanimously. And I'm sure Marilyn was relieved to get rid of our working title, *Not the Same Ol' Song and Dance*.

Then there was the other group of the "cooler" boys, who were very hard to reach in the beginning. We asked them all kinds of things, but either out of shyness or just because they were boys and couldn't be bothered, they had nothing to say. It was weird. I had never been stumped before in my reporting, but I couldn't get anything out of them. We first shot them playing basketball with their team after school. That, they didn't mind. Then, when it was over, we took them outside and . . . got nothing!

One day we did get something but not what we had intended. It was this same group of boys at the park. They were actually very goofy, and I just thought, Well this is a documentary and this is what we are getting. This is eleven! This is boy! And if it were anything but this, it would ring false. Boys were just going to be boys—at least in the beginning. This was, in fact, the essence of these boys this age—brilliantly subdued, painfully quiet, and sometimes just goofy.

There were other wonderful kids who provided us with great footage. There was the day we shot the kids dancing on the rocks. It was nice to get some of the kids who were not going to be competing and give them their day in the sun. I was happy when some of this footage (of kids who didn't make the dance team) made it into the movie. This rock shot went on to be the shot imprinted on many people's minds after seeing the movie. This was the alternative movie poster photo, rather than the tango pose photo that was eventually used, and it was powerful.

And, of course, once they were picked, there were the kids on the dance team. While there could be another book on just them, suffice it to say, they showed us what they're made of.

$\mathscr{T}$he weeks brought us from winter to spring and the competition loomed. The one thing P.S. 115 did (or, should I say, the principal did) was provide money to the team to buy matching outfits. It was a lot for these kids. In order for the *whole* team to get outfits, it had to be covered. While maybe ten of the twelve dancers could afford the outfit, one or two absolutely could not. This gave us the wonderful scene in which Yomaira and all the girls go shopping.

One of the funnier things about filming these kids was trying to find them! There was an unspoken "small worldliness" to Washington Heights, in the way that everyone seemed to know everyone else's business. When we were up there filming, it was just assumed we would know everything too. One little girl was quite upset that we had gone to her house to film her one Tuesday after school and missed her. "I'm at my aunt's house on Tucsdays," she scolded us. "Everyone knows that."

To get to their homes was a challenge. No one has an answering machine. The phone would ring and ring. We'd call and call and eventually we picked up on people's patterns, when they were home, and we eventually reached them. We had to work for access . . . physically. One day, I remember trying to find one of the kids and then I saw someone on the street yelling up five stories of the building to someone in a window and I thought, Aha! That's how you find someone!

MAKING YOU THINK!
THE STARS OF TRIBECA

*T*he TriBeCa kids showed us how hard it was to learn these dances, and how much actual concentration it took. They also didn't hesitate to let us hear about it. They were the wonderful, verbally astute, intellectually streetwise kids I have seen and known around this neighborhood for the past fifteen years. These were kids of savvy parents—not all wealthy, but mostly all educated. In most cases, both parents worked or chose to have professional careers. The divorce rate was high in this class (and probably reflected the rate in TriBeCa and other neighborhoods of similar means). Add to these demographics that this school was a very small, unique public school. These kids had been together, more or less—some moving, some coming on board— since Pre-K. With a small staff and such focused attention, it almost had the look and feel of an exclusive private school.

Allison was a contrast to Yomaira. I remember Marilyn saying something one day that really stuck with me. She said, "Allison has the luxury to cry." It was true. Compared with Yomaira, trying to give her kids a psychological kick in the pants with her driving words, Allison had the luxury to be a little more nurturing. The kids' futures were more secure. Allison was admired as a very caring teacher, and this showed.

The TriBeCa kids were open and warm from day one. When we first went to P.S. 150 to give an introduction and after the hour-long explanation of what we intended to do, one boy raised his hand and asked if we had a distribution deal in place! We said no, but if he knew anyone, we told him to work it for us.

These kids blew us away with their confidence and the conviction with which they spoke. Emma believed that women are the "advanced civilization." Zeb and his neighborhood buddy Mohammed admired girls for their "outer beauty" and their "inner beauty." One girl, Tara, took her team's loss to heart, starting what went on to be called the "cry fest." She worked hard at everything she did. This program could've been just something she had to get through because she was committed elsewhere all the time, but it wasn't. She genuinely wanted to win.

We had so many fun shoot days with these kids, just like we did in Washington Heights. In Washington Heights, we didn't really hang out at their homes much. There wasn't the room. We went to the neighborhood park and had to have the kids home before dark. With the TriBeCa kids, because they all lived in so many different places, even outside of TriBeCa, we got to spend more time with them in their own environments.

The scene that sums it all up for me with the TriBeCa kids was when they played in the local park in the sprinklers. I always see that scene as one all of those kids will watch throughout their lifetimes and remember the "good ol' days." In their neighborhood, in my neighborhood, that park is everyone's backyard and thus represents every TriBeCa kid's childhood.

MAKING YOU LAUGH!
THE STARS OF BENSONHURST

P.S. 112 in Bensonhurst was quaint and charming. It was there we got to know "the Basement Boys," Michael, Ronnie, and Donato. They were in the basement playing foosball and air hockey all the time. Marilyn was able to really get them talking. They started to unleash all their thoughts and dreams. They were the foosball philosophers, talking about their hopes for the future ("no one is poor"), girls and marriage ("girls just want to marry a millionaire but I'm not going to be one because it's the poor who are really rich, you know, and the rich are really poor," "yeah," "yeah"). They sing a love song and one boy reads us one of his poems.

We also shot the little Asian girls, Jai-Wen, Priscilla, Madeleine, and Tracy, on the porch discussing favorite dances and partners, feeding ants string cheese, talking about having long hair, and what's hard about being a woman. Priscilla says, "You *have* to be pregnant." I loved watching these girls dance in class, with their silky black hair in ponytails, all swinging the same gyration during the merengue, trying to move their hips.

On the days we didn't film, I still went to the classes to observe. As the weeks went on, I often had to step in as partner with one of the boys. That seemed to get great laughs out of all the kids. The boy was very, very nervous about putting his arms around me, and it was at that moment I realized just how hard it was for all of the kids. I thought it had to be easier to put his arms around me than some cute little girl in his class that he liked! The fear with which he placed that hand, or actually, let his hand hang on my waist like a dead fish, made me realize these kids were really achieving something big, really taking that step into adulthood. We persevered, and after four weeks, he was smiling and swinging, and I had (kind of) learned the foxtrot (well . . . okay . . . not really).

HOLDING ON TO THE TROPHY! THE STARS OF QUEENS

We didn't get to know the kids at P.S. 144 in Queens as well as we would have liked. But they were a group of beautiful, smart kids and the fact that their school's population was so diverse and the academic level so high made it interesting to watch them and hear what they had to say.

When competition time came, for the four schools and the kids we were filming, it was really no longer just about having fun and learning how to dance, or even learning the manners, courtesy, and respect so wonderfully espoused and reinforced by ABrT. It was now all about the competition. The buzz in every school gymnasium or classroom where thousands of little feet performed and practiced, over and over again, climbed up a couple notches every week prior to each competition. That excitement moved the story in a new direction. It became a story about winning.

ACTION PLAN

1. Know your subjects. What age are they? Think about and research that age group. For us, it was difficult to get some of the boys to talk. Had we looked into this a little more, we might have been able to reach them more effectively. Also, who you are and what you look like may affect how people act or what they say or don't say. One of the great things about filmmaking and/or reporting and the interviewing process is that it's a psychological challenge. You have to think about how things might get skewed based on all conditions.

2. Subtle contrasts make a great story. Obviously you have the story, at least in outline form, on paper prior to shooting and there must be some contrast or the story wouldn't have been interesting, but look for these contrasts while shooting your footage. People sur-

rounding your subjects often can and do add great depth to them and, if you're lucky, the storyline.

3. Find the comfort zone of respect for other people's privacy—and not only their comfort zone, but yours as a filmmaker. You have to be able to sleep later on knowing what you put out there and how it might affect those you chose to feature.

11

The Story Climax: The Competitions

*T*he brushstrokes are what actually happened in the story. To us it was one long, broad stroke, from having to learn the dances to getting to the final competitions. And when we got to the competitions, we decided to paint big and bold, making all that was going on splash across our canvas.

After the mandatory twenty classes were done and before the competitions began, a couple of the schools held intensive training sessions, some more than others. P.S. 150 in TriBeCa held a couple of sessions. We took a trip back to last year's winning school, P.S. 144 in Queens, to check out what they were up to only to find they were practicing almost every day after school. Yomaira in Washington Heights was cracking the whip over her team too, with intensive workouts held wherever they could find space. It became very clear that those who wanted it were willing to work for it.

It was during these intensive training sessions that we realized the teams that would get beyond the first competitions would be the ones that were putting in the extra time. The fact that the teams that were putting in the extra time had strong and committed teachers who were invested in guiding the process also became very obvious. For those final nine teams that would eventually grace the big stage in less than three weeks' time there was a commonality among all of them; they wanted it.

Yomaira's intensive practices continued every day in the weeks leading up to the competitions. There is a scene in which she has a "dance-off" with one of the girls. This scene hit me, as a forty-something mother, pretty hard and close to home. To me it was a window into Yomaira as a young woman and the beauty she exuded. While it wasn't anywhere near symbolizing the passing of a baton, it definitely symbolized something— possibly one's fleeting youth and another's fleeting innocence all on one dance floor.

There were two to three quarterfinals in each borough, then one semifinal, which then brought nine teams to the finals held at the World Financial Center's Winter Garden. While we were filming only the competitions in which our featured schools competed, I attended every competition to find out who was advancing. I wanted to talk to and inform the teachers and some of the parents about our doc and get releases from those kids who would be advancing to the next competition and in front of our camera, so that when we were ready to roll, everything was in order.

We had two cameras rotating on and off the dance floor at each of the quarterfinal and semifinal competitions. The on-floor camera would capture the dancing and the off-floor camera would gather audience reactions. At the finals, it was a four-camera shoot because only one camera was allowed on the stage at a time. Two cameras rotated on and off the stage and in the pits—the teams' holding areas. Another camera was on the audience, primarily on our teams' families. The fourth camera was stationary on a stand focused on the stage and was hooked up to the event sound system. All other cameras had their own sound units.

THE BROOKLYN
QUARTERFINALS

*T*he first shot of the P.S. 112 kids walking to the competition pretty much set the mood of that shoot. Everyone is so dressed up! During the quarterfinals we watched the Bensonhurst kids counting mistakes. Michael has an encounter with a tall girl (and she with him!) and his father chimes in, "It doesn't matter how tall. You did really good!"

During the tango, Priscilla and Michael dance right behind the judges, who almost fall over them. Nobody remembers escort position when they get called up to accept their ribbons. They investigate the gift bags and then the Bensonhurst kids realize they didn't move on to the semifinals. There was genuine surprise.

We went back and filmed what we called the "Aftermath," to record the Bensonhurst kids' feelings about the whole experience. We gathered the team in their library. Priscilla, the voice of reason, and sometimes the voice of doom, couldn't seem to get past how many mistakes they made, though they still got a "silver" place (that is, second place; there were no third places and only the first place—or "gold"—winners continued on to the next level). The other kids kind of spoke in circles and tried to justify why they felt good about it all. Michael (known now as "Tango Face"), jumped in, going as far as saying that he thought the competition should've been harder. After talking about dancing with the "girl who was like an adult," he said, "I guess we didn't want to win. We just wanted to have fun. If we wanted to win, we would've tried harder. But we didn't want to . . . try harder."

In the edit, we included the scene of P.S. 112's school orchestra, with a lot of the same kids who were taking ballroom dancing, right before we filmed the Aftermath. We did this to show that this charming school, these amazing kids, really just enjoyed everything they did, whether they did it well or not, and that helped to reinforce the main message this team delivered: that sometimes it's just enough to have fun.

THE MANHATTAN QUARTERFINALS

In Bensonhurst, the kids all got ready at home and then met at a corner and walked together. With prep time for the Manhattan quarterfinals, we actually got to hang out and film at the school while the TriBeCa kids got ready. This was a lot of fun. The TriBeCa kids were all excited and feeling really good about getting dressed up. The girls wiggled in their dresses and the boys stood taller in their suits and ties.

The kids who were not competing were there too. Everyone was pumped. The crew had grins ear to ear. It was raining and they left the school and headed to the subway for the competition. They didn't have to, but the team held the escort position all the way. On the subway, much to our amusement, they broke into song—"Lean on Me."

The TriBeCa team got to P.S. 11, where the Manhattan quarterfinals were held. They prepped in the cafeteria, fixing their sashes and hair, and working on assigning the dances. The competition began and the team's camaraderie was very obvious and spellbinding. The girls, without missing a beat, mouthed the words to "Fever" by Peggy Lee. (I remember the music publisher didn't want to give us this song because of the risqué lyrics possibly not being appropriate for eleven-year-olds and my reply was "They don't listen to the words.")

After really giving it their all, the TriBeCa team missed the opportunity to go on to the semifinals by just three points. Cyrus, the boy with the curly hair and the big thoughts, questions Pierre about the point system. The scene ends with the major cry fest. Claudia was in and out, holding on them like a pro. Our second cameraman just stood as still as a predator in a bush and held the shot on the kids. A couple of adults asked us to pull the cameras, and while Marilyn and I were aware that we had a potential "situation" on our hands, the DPs gave it room to breathe, as did Marilyn and I. I had to hide behind a pole because the whole situation was so devastating and I myself was close to tears. It was tense but what a moment captured! Those feelings pouring up and out of those kids and onto the floor and hence, into the film. It was then you could see how much advancing on to the semifinals had meant to them. It certainly broke our hearts at the time.

At their Aftermath, their teacher asks the kids if there is anything they want to talk about. There is obviously some resentment about losing. Tara talks about having done everything right, including "eye to eye contact," and still doesn't understand how if they did everything right, they could lose. While the Bensonhurst kids reminded us to have fun, the TriBeCa kids reminded us that sometimes it is also necessary to feel humility. They experienced firsthand that even if you do everything right, sometimes you don't get what you want. This is possibly one of the first "injustices" we all learn hopping over the fence of puberty to become a young adult, and TriBeCa showed us this with raw courage and very real, uncensored emotions.

SEMIFINALS

*W*ashington Heights' P.S. 115, because they placed so high last year in the finals, were given a bye to advance right to the semifinals. They had an extra week of intensive training.

On the day of the semifinals, we again had two cameras. Claudia started at the school with the kids and our second cameraman met us at the competition. On the way to the subway, Yomaira questions Wilson about not dancing full force. He replies that he's saving himself for the competition. Elsamelys was sick all morning and didn't know if she could dance, but she ended up rising to the occasion. Yomaira was noticeably nervous. The girls do a cheer on the train (the same cheer they end up saying onstage after they win the final competition). The crew could never understand all the words but I think they mention "kicking your ass," so we never asked for the words. They get to the school in Chelsea (the same school where the Manhattan quarterfinals were held), and the girls immediately retreat to the bathroom, where they proceed, for an hour, to put more gook, gel, foam and spray, and pink stuff in big jars in their hair, more than anyone could ever believe!

Yomaira gave the girls last-minute tips and the competition began. We had great shots of Yomaira dancing in the audience, hugging the column in excitement, the boys getting into it and the girls crossing fingers and holding hands. The "flashovers" during the dances were emotive and moved the story along. It wasn't as if they didn't encounter problems. They were feeling the heat.

It was now obvious, at the semifinals, the *real* competition had begun. Elsamelys, who had such a bad tummy ache an hour before, gave us one half of the scene of all scenes. She and Wilson took the floor and did the rumba. He does his turn, adding his own touch to the dance, the hand to the lower chest "matador" move, and she spins around with that look on her face. Many later said they couldn't remember the last time something in a movie made them cheer like that, many lifting up out of their seats with enthusiasm. This is the one defining moment in the film that played universally, the same way, in every country, in every language. The Washington Heights team's path at that moment was clear.

Marilyn and I were thrilled. Over the life of the whole production, there wasn't a time we were worried about the story, but on that day, we both looked at each other, knowing that if P.S. 115 from Washington Heights did not go on to the finals, it would end up a completely different story. In those last few hours when Washington Heights danced, it became about winning a place in the finals. Marilyn and I were standing in the back, behind the crowds, sweating. Washington Heights moved on to the finals, and needless to say, we were excited—and quite relieved.

THE FINALS

*B*y the time the finals rolled around, we had four cameras ready to roll. Claudia started with P.S. 115 up in Washington Heights. The girls on the team had their hair done in the library by several moms. We got a great shot of the girls looking in the mirror in total awe of how pretty they looked.

Yomaira tells the kids that if they want to bring any food or water, they should buy it in Washington Heights because downtown is too expensive. I met them at the subway exit on Chambers Street in TriBeCa. The team walked over to the Winter Garden.

It is on this walk that the kids notice the big hole in the ground where the World Trade Center once stood. There were some full-circle moments at this point in our story as the principal of P.S. 150 in TriBeCa had pointed out at the beginning of the movie that 9/11 had just happened and her classes had just moved back into their building. It showed the passage of time.

Upstairs in a holding room, all nine teams were sectioned off, each getting ready. The Washington Heights boys and girls of P.S. 115 were putting on a fashion show, showing off how they could actually walk and maneuver the catwalk. The boys shared a bottle of men's cologne, which prompted the dance teacher's hilarious comment, "It's not important to look good, but to smell good." The girls checked and sprayed their own hair, and then went after the boys to do the same to their hair. Rodney, the dance teacher, reminds them to tuck their shirts in—"all the way in"—something he does at the very beginning of the movie. (I guess some things just can't be learned.) These moments bring the viewer to a place where what they saw at the beginning now loops perfectly well into the lead-up to the end. We were starting to bring closure to our story and indicated this with reflective statements and scenes.

At the same time, P.S. 144 from Queens arrived in cars and at the most elegant entrance. Our second DP got an amazing shot when the kids come through the revolving doors and head up the escalators. The teacher of P.S. 144 also supplied some last-minute tips and reminders.

It was quite a sight to see: nine teams, beautiful girls and handsome boys. In addition to all the sashes secured, hair fixed, and lip gloss applied, the mother ship of ABrT brought homemade sandwiches so all the kids would have something to eat before the competition. There was a kind of homespun feeling behind the scenes at the event. All the hard work of ABrT's Dancing Classrooms came down to this one night's event.

Yomaira dispensed hugs and kisses as the kids paraded across the floor to take their places in the holding area on the side of the stage. The sun setting west beyond the river was so bright that early evening, it made our audience shots difficult to get as it was shining right in their eyes, not to mention it was difficult for them to see their kids dance. The judges were well known. Some were world famous ballroom dancers. Out of the seven hundred release forms collected, the hardest to get were the releases from the judges. It was not until the day of the finals that I secured the last two of the five judges' release forms. It felt like such a relief to have accomplished getting all those releases. The end to that task was an indicator that our production was nearing completion, as there were no more releases to obtain. The primary filming, while there would be some follow-up shoot days, was basically coming to an end. What a great culminating event to also help us mark our finish.

The dancing was awesome. When the camera scans the parents' faces, they are so proud. The fans are extremely exuberant, and I loved that there was all this emotion and physical investment in what was happening and what had been happening for the last four months.

By the time the final dance-off came into play, after the three gold teams had been chosen, there was never a question of who would prevail. We could feel it. The audience, again, rose to their feet and broke out with spontaneous cheering and clapping. Washington Heights wins the grand prize. The girls give a cheer and the boys raise up that giant trophy in the Stanley Cup tradition in hockey. A look at the audience, Washington Heights' P.S. 115 fans, showed all that "behave yourself" had been tossed out the window. The adults threw confetti up in the air and jumped for joy. There were some grumblings about this behavior by others, but a janitor, cleaning up the mess, seemed to get it right when he said, "They won, for God sakes. Give them their moment."

ACTION PLAN

1. Success is in the details. No one cares about your project as *much* as you—the filmmaker or filmmakers. Along with that, no one cares about doing all the little things. If they start to unravel, or you lose control, you'll work twice as hard to get it back on track.

   We had a skeletal crew and only hired production assistants (PAs) for the competitions, when we had multiple cameras. Other than that, we juggled it all and not only for budgetary purposes but also because we didn't have time. We were on a tight production schedule because the program to the final competition was a finite time period and we also wanted to get this movie out in a timely fashion because next year's program was right around the corner, and kids grow fast. So there were many duties of which we had to stay on top. Not that I would recommend this to new filmmakers. You should hire a PA, or a few. I suppose I felt that with the amount of money we were responsible for, Marilyn and I had to control a lot of the things happening. I'm sure that I took on more than I should have, just based on this fear of losing control. A natural neurosis, no doubt, in indie film-making.

There were permits, insurance, setting up vendors, and a ton of things to get in order. Brian was clutch in all these things. Marilyn logged all the footage shot and made the next day's shot list, looked at dailies, made notes for Sabine, and updated the shoot log. I took on a lot of the physical functions to gear up for the next day and called to schedule future shoots or confirm the next day's shoots. We both updated questions and discussed strategy about interviews. And everyone pitched in on transcribing interviews.

Here's a short list broken down on a daily basis and then also on an as-needed basis. You can figure it out. Obviously, it's to be divvied up by your team.

a. Get all film permits and insurance in order.

b. Secure lighting and camera vendors.

c. Charge batteries the night before each shoot.

d. The production bag should include everything you can think of, as if you are on your way to your first day of kindergarten: scissors, tape (all kinds!), clips, pens, pencils, Post-its, pain relievers (all kinds), a digital camera, Windex, paper towels, wipes, rubber bands, string, glue, batteries, and any necessary toiletries! Anything you can think of that someone might say, "Hey, do we have any . . ."—bring it.

e. Check the weather to be aware and bring appropriate supplies (umbrellas and plastic bags for rainy outdoor shoots).

f. Gather crew.

g. Review shot list for the day.

h. Get to locations on time.

i. Get the footage.

j. Make sure crew is fed (and feed them well, they are working very hard!).

k. Get more footage.

l. Have a back-up plan (b-roll list) in case plans change (and expect that they will).

m. At the end of the day, transfer your miniDVs onto DVDs, but you must have this capability on your DVD player or else do it at the dubbing house. (See item p.) We transferred onto VHS tapes at the time because DVDs were too expensive. It's changed now, but I still prefer VHS.

n. Recharge the camera batteries for the next day's shoot.

o. Make notes of the footage you are taping for the editor. You'll start to log topics, ideas, threads, and themes as you watch.

p. Take the original tapes (they now equal GOLD) to a dubbing house and make copies. (This way, if you happen to accidentally throw one down the garbage chute in a discarded empty Barbie toy carton like I did, you won't want to kill yourself.)

q. From the dailies (VHS tapes), you will record your shoot log—every scene and key statements.

r. You can either hire a transcriber or, if you are insane, like our team, you will do it yourselves! While in the edit, you sometimes have to find specific lines or phrases, and you can search the interviews for dialogue you need.

s. If foreign languages are spoken in your film, like ours, dialogue also has to be translated after it is transcribed.

t. Keep updating your outline and other documents that help you to define your story and your mission. You might consider expanding your outline to a treatment now if your story is pretty solid. You might want to devise a mega-shot wish list, a flowchart of leading characters, a report of investigation (what now needs to be researched), and always update your list of questions for your subjects. This changes over time and certainly changes if your doc has moved in another direction. All of these things help to keep up with where the doc is now headed.

u. Fund-raising—don't forget to keep the money coming in so you can keep the doc in production.

v. Keep thinking about the music aspect—not only clearing, but begin to look into composers for the score.

w. Equipment upkeep. Keep it all clean and running soundly.

x. Minivan or crew van upkeep. Track gas and mileage expenses.

y. Desk duties, including release forms, accounts payable, tax issues, and upkeep.

z. Production supplies replenishment—most important, tape stock.

aa. Still photography maintenance.

bb. Write thank-you notes to crew, vendors, anyone who is helping you out. A doc takes on the soul of its collective community. Be good in return.

2. If you can delegate any of the tasks listed above or have enough in the budget to pay a PA or PM (produc-

tion assistant or production manager), do so. For the tasks I handled this time, I didn't, because I wanted to get my hands "dirty" with every step of the process. It was the only way I was going to learn the whole process, and I felt it would be the only way I would be able to delegate those tasks effectively the next time if I so chose.

3. Always follow your subject until he/she or they all are either putting their heads down to sleep or shutting the door on you. Don't end up with the "shot that got away." We had one of those but it's too painful to talk about.

4. Enjoy production and gathering the footage. While it seems very hard at the time, as you look back at the arc of your filmmaking process, it will be the period that you will remember most fondly.

12

Editing and Postproduction

*I*n July 2004, Marilyn and I were notified that we were selected as a "Work-in-Progress" for the Spotlight on Documentary section of the twenty-sixth IFP Market and Conference. The
IFP (Independent Feature Project) is a nonprofit organization
that fosters filmmakers and supports independent filmmaking.
They have this New York City–based market every year to bring
the filmmakers and distributors together. We had submitted a
five-minute piece about a month earlier. We had to start building a strategy for the IFP Market but, more important, we now
had to put together the whole product. We had to have a film.

Now Sabine really started to dive into the primary editing
phase of shaping the story. We had to have a twenty-minute
piece cut to show at the September IFP Market and we were
shooting for a rough cut by mid-August to submit to festivals.
The deadline for the Sundance Film Festival was early September, and it was October for the Berlin International Film
Festival.

Through the course of observing and getting the footage

over the four-month period, it became apparent that our story was starting to head in a different direction. The daily shoots had affected this too. All the ideas and thoughts that were discussed and debated had shaped the story during shooting. Now Marilyn and Sabine would begin to shape the story in the editing room. There was another story, or perhaps the same story, in our case, wanting to be told a different way, and this was when it started to happen. What had seemed logical on paper or what had been outlined to make sense in words, originally, now would be taken into another dimension, an even higher dimension, to be placed onto another platform, into another medium, a story where the images and how they were presented said it all.

Marilyn's idea from the beginning was not to use a narrator, but to tell the story through the voices of the characters. This made cutting the film more complicated, but she knew that it would make it play out more like a feature and less like a traditional documentary. This is what I had wanted from the start. It was very exciting to me.

After principal photography, Marilyn and Sabine had started to outline the flow of the story. Sabine had found a great way to condense time by skipping from school to school within the same dance lesson, which was brilliant, because there was so much repetition, yet we needed to represent each school progressing through the dance course. The story was outlined scene by scene onto an Excel document. From there it was transferred onto index cards, scene by scene, color-coded by school. The montages each had their own color. As Sabine refined the cut, the cards would then be rearranged on the wall and used to insert montages, change the order of scenes, and sometimes eliminate scenes altogether. Looking at the film laid out in this way helped us see the flow very clearly, how often each school was coming up, and what logically ensued.

Sabine was the first to recognize that the adults fell away—almost all of them. All the footage we had of every personal interview of the dance teachers, the judges, Yvonne and Pierre, the principals, and the teachers was not on the front burner anymore. The "cast of characters" unfolded and, as if in a slow bloom, brought the movie into focus—a story told, and thus driven, by the kids. And the harmony of this happening reminded me of a magical moment when the story unfolded from the kids' perspectives, and this move now had complete and total synergy with the focus of the edit.

The initial assembly was a little over five hours long and was finished by the middle of July. Marilyn and I took a look at this cut in Marilyn's living room one Saturday afternoon. It seemed impossible that we would be able to lose more than half of this material. We had some decisions to make. Not to mention that I felt a little queasy. This was a humbling procedure. I was not adept at looking at rough cuts. This takes very trained eyes. Additionally, we had shot our footage and were so crazy excited about it all and now we had to squish it down and pack it into a finite amount of space, a finite amount of time. We had to put boundaries on the soul of our project.

What we gathered from this cut was a fat presentation of the story. We had to decide how we would narrow it. To me, there was never a question that if I was going to make that "Just-One" movie, I wanted it on the big screen. Theatrical release. We had to see whether this was realistic or not. Marilyn wanted theatrical release, too, so at least we were both working toward the same goal and would work hard on trying to get there.

We discussed whether it might not be best formatted as a series. It had all the components. We had a lot of material to spread out over a possible episodic television show or PBS series. But we had so much wanted theatrical release. On the other hand, if we chose to make it into a feature-length film, a lot of material would be cut. We had a *lot* of material. We had four teams, the American Ballroom Theater, all the teachers and principals, and the various scenes from each neighborhood. What I kept thinking about, in actuality, were these tiny characters who played "larger than life," doing this quiet yet elegant thing, ballroom dancing, in their regular street clothes, that was not even a thought in their heads four months ago. As Cyrus, the boy from TriBeCa, says in the movie when asked about ballroom dancing and the foxtrot during one of our interviews, "If you think about it, ballroom dancing is like this tiny little thing. A tiny little grain of sand if you count the entire country." It was the oxymoron of this small nugget of the idea and everything it entailed, this glimpse into a little slice-of-life story, being huge and in your face, right there up on the big screen, that was so mesmerizing. The audience is *in their* world—the wondrous world of the kids.

After a long discussion Marilyn and I decided that theatrical it would be.

Because of our decision for theatrical release, there was an issue of fitting the amount of material that we had into that finite theatrical-release time period for a doc—85 to 120 minutes. We discussed just telling P.S. 115's story, but the decision to nix this was just as quick for me as the one about theatrical release. I wanted to show all three schools, along with the flashback to the fourth school, P.S. 144 in Queens. I don't think seeing P.S. 115 in Washington Heights and getting to know those kids would be as effective without meeting the kids from TriBeCa, Bensonhurst, and Queens, too. I'm sure it would have been interesting, but it would have been a different movie. Not the one we had envisioned after Marilyn's idea to follow more than one school way back in the beginning. These edit-driven issues are significant not only from an artistic standpoint, which is most important, but also from a business standpoint. It could take the project on a different path regarding sales and marketing of the movie. All these aspects must be thought out and discussed so that the most logical, practical, effective, and, of course, artistic choice is made.

Having this long assembly was a major accomplishment. It was the first emergence of our piece from beginning to end. Now it was a matter of telling this story with fewer scenes, shorter scenes. Over the next month, Sabine and Marilyn took that five-hour piece and started to sculpt it. Favorite scenes went a-flyin'! Cut. Finito. It had to be done. There were tough decisions on what to lose and how to dramatically cut it back. Many things that we initially thought were crucial to the story were cut out. Many things that we all loved, or that we individually loved, were taken out. The beloved montages were dramatically cut back and, in many cases, eliminated. This was hard but necessary. We had to make difficult choices. The questions we had to ask ourselves when considering cutting particular scenes were "Is the scene necessary to the story?" "Does it provide information needed to help move the story along?" "If not, what is its purpose then—comedic? To pull on heartstrings? Or just a perfect visual—a second of candy for the eyes?"

Marilyn had said that the funny thing about editing is that often something is cut out and you don't even miss it. The story, if strong, still tells itself. This turned out to be very true. There are many times we try to remember a funny scene that we cut and when we do finally remember it, while it's still funny to us in an abstract way, it really seems to be out of place now when thinking about the flow of the movie, the telling of the story.

By the time we had our first screening, the cut was two and a half hours long. By the time we premiered at our first film festival, it was one hour and fifty-five minutes. The final cut runs at one hour and forty-four minutes.

We wanted to add some music behind it. Marilyn had thought long and hard about the feeling and movement of the scenes and for our purposes at this point, she decided on the score from *American Beauty*, which is a Thomas Newman composition. It fit perfectly. She also put that great Verve song at the end but though I never wanted it to go, we were maxed out in the budget music-wise already and the song (come on, you know it! "Bittersweet Symphony") was clearly overused at the time, so we cut it. We cleaned it up a bit, transferred it to a digibeta (a higher-quality tape that accommodates the whole film), and set off to hold a couple screenings to get input. We invited industry people and close friends to the screening. Sabine, Claudia, Marilyn, and I got an earful of specific opinions, details, and suggestions. Sabine taught me how to listen to critics at this level: to listen for the big things (the story line, continuity, flow, structure) and not the little things (put in more of that kid, more shots of the feet, change that song, and so on). It was an interesting process and we listened closely and made appropriate changes based, as always, on crew consensus. I was adamant about always getting everyone's input and firm about the decision-making process being democratic. With this type of collaboration, everyone's opinion mattered.

As we continued to fine-tune the film with both the edit and the quality of output with regard to picture and sound, we also had to replace the temporary music score. This is a separate, time-consuming job, and while most filmmakers leave it until the end, it's the first thing filmmaking books *and* other filmmakers will tell you not to put off until last. We started working with a couple of experienced and talented musicians to compose and orchestrate an original score and the end song. Marilyn spearheaded this function. It was extremely stressful for her all the way through and I got a taste of it in the end. It was challenging to replace Thomas Newman's score and that *great* Verve song, but our composers did a super job. Marilyn also came up with the idea for an originally composed end song named after the title of the movie—*Mad Hot Ballroom.* The composer worked dialogue from the movie into the song. While I had wanted the end song to be a combination of swing and hip-hop, representing the morphing of what went on in the movie between the young kids and the "old" music, Marilyn had envisioned more of a classic song, more swing, to keep in pace and feel with the other songs in the film. For my sake, she had the composers add some hip-hop beats to the song to let me hear how it would sound, and it really detracted from it. She also had in mind a male voice to sing the song, and I had wanted a Macy Gray–type female voice (we had so few women singing on the soundtrack—Peggy Lee and Della Reese being the only women out of eighteen songs). We heard some samples of men singing the song and it just didn't sound right. In one night, with one phone call, we heard the amazing voice of Tina Fabrique and we had our singer. The song was and is so right and fitting that many people to this day don't know that it is a new song composed for the movie. They think it's a classic from the forties or fifties and that we named the movie *after* the song!

At this point, we started to figure out the next steps, starting with attending the IFP Market, which opened the door to the industry for us to begin the process of marketing our film. What would happen at the IFP Market would end up being the beginning of a quintessential Cinderella story in the doc world—and our world, for that matter. And you can bet that Marilyn and I were not even thinking about finding dresses for any ball or thinking about that seemingly out-of-reach glass slipper. We were too busy with our sleeves rolled up trying to finish the movie—as finished as it could be.

ACTION PLAN

1. Confirmation of casting your big net while shooting comes when you see how much footage you have to get to create the movie you want. While you'd think that you'd like to shoot more efficiently next time, it doesn't work that way. You need all the footage to get those sequences. It turned out that we did shoot efficiently because we had a firm story line to follow. If your doc doesn't have a finite story or time frame, be careful and map out your plan as best you can, or it will get costly.

2. It is quite obvious that you should have a director and editor who know what they are doing. The editing process is creative, complicated, challenging, and probably the most crucial and significant aspect of documentary filmmaking. It is where the movie becomes what it is to be.

3. Based on what you have at this point, think about where you want it to go from an artistic and storytelling aspect (being realistic, of course, but not compromising).

4. From a business perspective, evaluate the marketing fit and placement of the film.

5. Show your movie and get input. You are going to have audiences. This is what you want. So take a deep breath and show it. Try not to react to their reactions, just listen. Discuss the issues later with your core crew and decide what your changes, if any, will be.

6. It's important to remember that the score is another piece of the movie. It's a part of its soul. Start working on the music component early.

13

Sales and Marketing
of the Unsold Film

*O*nce we reached this stage in the edit, the other components that came into focus involved research on the market and the marketing of the film. We had to think about how we were going to initially get the film "out there." There are film markets such as the IFP that connect the filmmaker with the key players in the industry. We were ready and raring to go at this market. We had a poster and postcards designed and printed with the intention to promote our film's presence there.

There are film festivals. Now we're talking! I had come full circle when it came back to figuring out exactly which festivals we would want to try to enter. Film festivals are not only fun but one of the most effective ways to get your film noticed. The first thing I did was read *The Ultimate Film Festival Survival Guide*. Marilyn and I narrowed it down to the top ten we hoped to attend. She had an idea of where our movie might be a good fit. I then researched all the festival Web sites, read their requirements, and downloaded their applications. We focused only on the festivals that fit with our topic and style of documentary because there are a lot of festivals and you have to condense it somehow. Some festivals are also very specific about what they accept. Many festivals have reputations for accepting a certain style of documentary (for example, "edgy," which our film was not). I filled out film festival applications ahead of time and got everything ready so that when we had a fine cut (the cut after the rough cut and the one before the finished film), we could have VHS copies made and sent out according to each festival's deadline. Take notice: filling out festival applications is like filling out college admissions applications. I printed out the former year's Sundance Film Festival application and started to write select pieces that were requested and put together all the components that were required. The point is to allot the right amount of time to do this accurately. You also have to submit your rough or fine cut. Everyone says never rush to finish your film to make the deadline of a festival (and to this day, I have never met a filmmaker who is *not* rushing to make a festival deadline if they are close to finishing a film). To say having a producer's rep or sales agent attached is helpful is a complete and utter understatement. If you can get one, it can make all the difference in the world.

We had also started investigating another way to get the movie out there and noticed—"four-walling." This is where the filmmaker rents the theater for a couple days and nights to show the film. You have to promote the film yourself (there are some very good art-house theaters that will help you to do this) with the goal of selling as many tickets as you can to bring in your audience. The worst that could happen is you'd at least be able to submit the film for an Oscar nomination, as this is one of the requirements to be met by the Academy for all unsold films (*Balseros* in 2004 got an Oscar nod this way). It was here that I tried to go back to Target Corporation and get them involved in a four-walling campaign in all fifty states to benefit arts in education organizations in each state. Nothing ever came of it but we had kept this option in our back pocket as a last resort.

There were several other sales and marketing tools and promotion pieces that we designed for the IFP market and future film festivals. We created a one-page marketing-oriented fact sheet to pass out with our synopsis. This should include what your movie is about, why it's relevant, why someone should see your film, and why they should care—obviously not all titled this way. Be creative, write it well, and get the attention of acquisition executives or film sales agents. We didn't have a trailer cut to hand out because that would get expensive. But if you make one, by all means, pass it out. We also never had an original Web site for the film.

Some filmmakers also do some zany and crazy promotions or pass out some wacky things that may be befitting of their films, but we didn't see the need, nor did we want to do this. The closest we came to something like this was thinking up a series of cards with the kids on the front, similar to baseball trading cards, but we decided not to overcomplicate this effort. We were very keen on having one message, one image, come through, knowing this would be most effective.

Besides thinking up marketing and promotion angles, there is some other market and industry business information that it pays to stay on top of. For example, many movies and topics are trended. If there were four movies out about the president the prior year, it would be pretty tough to try to sell your "president" movie this year, unless you had a genuinely fresh angle or exciting new approach. Our real competition were other dance movies and certainly any other movie about ballroom dancing or kids doing something different. Busy industry executives are basically looking to find the next big hit or hits coming down the pipeline. So having a topic that will prove marketing-worthy and relevant six months or a year from now is a very good thing. Personally, I think that these days many docs, at least for theatrical release, have to have a very high relevancy to the times. They need to be based on something that is happening in the world (Gore's *An Inconvenient Truth;* Moore's *Fahrenheit 9/11*) or on a rising trend (our *Mad Hot Ballroom*), or have a built-in marketing angle, strategy, or (bite my lip) gimmick. While both the IFP and festivals are great avenues for filmmakers, they are even better resources for the industry, as they serve to gather all potentially great products into one place for buying entities looking for quality content or perhaps the "next, best, biggest."

It is also important to make sure you have a strong selling platform. Be on message—meaning, find your one hook line, the reason and purpose of your film, and get it down to one sentence—and stick with it. When we came up with our own logline, it seemed we were right on target: "Ordinary Kids. An Extraordinary Journey." It pretty much summed it up. And we stuck with the one image of the two kids locked in tango formation on the rocks.

A great thing to do is to look at similar films and where they ended up in the market. Better yet, study the promotional materials (posters, Web sites) of movies *you* love or that were successful to see what you like and don't like and how they executed or presented things: Where is the emphasis? What is the layout like? Is it effective? Does it catch your eye? Act like a consumer and not a filmmaker and see what you need to *see* and then do it.

The biggest overall obstacle to bringing a product such as a film "to market" is that there is no way to prove it will work or sell. With other products, those that are tangible items, there is market testing. But with movies, you are investigating your market—looking for your shelf space, if you will—even before you have a finished product. It's a bit like hawking air for a while. You are selling an idea. It's your vision of what this film can be that you are placing. Just work as hard as possible to make sure your product comes close to matching what you're selling and pray that the market, whatever is going on out there in the world, and how all this fits with your film, comes up on your side. I hate to use a cliché, but timing *is* everything.

I read in a filmmaking book that you should never show anyone in the industry a rough cut—it is better to wait and then premiere the film at a film festival. We followed this advice. Similar to the mentality at a real estate open house, it is the one chance you have to create a big splash in the market, create some buzz, and hopefully attract a buyer.

ACTION PLAN

1. Begin research on the market and marketing the film. How are you going to get your film "out there"?

2. There are film markets and film festivals. Do your research and check them out.

3. Investigate "four-walling"—you never know.

4. Devise a sales and marketing strategy and a list of all the marketing and promotional pieces you will want to design, produce, and distribute.

5. Many movies and topics are trended. Think about who your competition is.

6. Think about timing.

7. Make sure you have a strong selling platform. Be on message—find your one hook line, the reason and purpose of your film, and get it down to one sentence—and stick with it.

8. Study the marketing and promotional materials of similar movies, movies you love, movies that are successful.

9. Look at other films similar to yours—learn how they were marketed, what their messages were, and where they ended up in the market.

10. Don't show anyone in the industry a rough cut unless he or she is a sales agent or, obviously, the group of people who make up the film festival submission review boards.

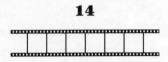

14

Mad Hot Ballroom's
Unusual Ride

THE IFP MARKET

$\mathscr{P}$rior to the conference, the IFP sends out a catalog to all distributors and they get to read the synopses of the participating films. If they so choose, they can schedule a one-on-one meeting with the filmmakers. It's very much like speed dating. We got a list of entities interested about a month before the market—there were eleven entities that wanted to meet with us, from HBO and the IFC to the major network station in Finland. The Finns are world-renowned for their good taste in film and their obsession with docs. Needless to say, we were psyched. The interest was there.

We headed into the New York City–based conference in September 2004, and while there were conferences and panels on grants, music clearing, festivals, and distribution, many of which I attended, my mind was elsewhere. I was more interested in watching the happenings around me. Similar to any major industry conference, it was buzzing with energy, but the difference here was the collection of creative people who write, produce, and direct the latest, greatest, hippest entertainment. They were the industry movers, people who had the ability and power to put any and all creative endeavors into a tangible marketed presence, to get it out there and get the job done. There were filmmakers going everywhere all the time. There were acquisitions people, distributors, the inside "gang," either in the library or in some special lounge where they could gather without being continuously sought after by the filmmakers. Every time one of the distributors came out, he or she would be swarmed by filmmakers. This was happening in numerous locations around the conference site.

Though the busiest place was outside the theaters in the lobby, our two screenings were actually anticlimactic. I think fewer than twenty people showed up for each one, and half were our friends. Most of the acquisition execs went to the IFP library and viewed the movies that way. It was more efficient for them. However, it was cool to see our movie up on a big screen in a theater we'd love to be in one day.

The one-on-one meetings were great. We had to pitch our film several times. I felt like I was in my twenties again, interviewing for my first job. It was interesting to meet everyone but I hated the process too. At the time, it was hard sitting there with executives from HBO, IFC, or PBS talking about what a great movie we thought we had. Everyone else was doing this too. What truly was going to make any of these people, who had our fate right there in the palms of their hands for ten minutes, think our film was the one they should buy? It was both stressful and a little humiliating, to say the least. While you can sit there and say what amounts to just a mouthful of words, it is your product that ends up speaking for itself. It's the film that is the end-all and be-all in this whole scheme of things.

Shortly after the pitch meetings, Marilyn was talking about how, with regard to film distributors, small is nice and small is good, when my cell phone rang. Marilyn had just said that since we had a "little" movie, it would be nice to not get involved with a huge distributor who might want to take it over and make all kinds of cuts or edits. And since we were dealing with kids, I had never intended to give any entity final creative control.

I answered my phone. It was the vice president of acquisitions from a major studio asking if she could see the rough cut of *Mad Hot Ballroom*.

"Never show anyone a rough cut" rang through my head. The rationale being that if one large, influential entity passes on your film, the others might follow suit. I paused, kind of choking or swallowing hard or both. I think Marilyn was still babbling on about "small" and I said, "Can we call you back with an answer?" There was a long pause and then she said, "Sure." I told her we'd call back in ten minutes. When I hung up my cell, I turned to Marilyn and said, "Is this studio small enough for you?" as I told her this very large studio's name.

We proceeded to jump up and down, which I distinctly remember because I had bought these stupid, great-looking, very fashionable boots (pointy toes!) and my feet were killing me. We jumped and screamed, knowing we were screaming and looking stupid, so we tempered it to whimpering, muffled screams. We stopped and looked at each other.

I said, "What do you want to do?"

She said, "I don't know."

We waited exactly ten minutes to see if any otherworldly signs came up. None did. My gut told me not to show them anything. I told Marilyn this, and she agreed. I dialed the number back. Marilyn held my arm. I scrunched my face up tight, hoping that if this was the wrong move, a cab would accidentally hit a pothole, veer out of control, and hit me, making the phone fly from my hand so I couldn't make the call.

No cab. No hit. It rang. The call went through. We politely declined showing a rough cut, clarified our intention of premiering at a film festival, thanked her profusely for even being interested in us, and ended the call. Marilyn and I just stared at each other for a long, long time. We turned and walked in silence. There was no more talk about "small" and "right fit." We were churning it over in our heads, wondering privately, separately, if we had just screwed up. It was a sinking, horrible feeling.

My phone rang. It was the same woman. She said something that would chart the course of our movie, and our lives, forever: "If you won't let me see a rough cut, would you at least allow me to recommend you to a sales agent? You ladies really have something, and you should be protected out there." She recommended a sales agent. We showed the agent our rough cut eventually, and things took off from there.

Once we signed on with the agent, it was like we had stepped into that golden carriage that used to be our pumpkin. I'm not talking about Town Cars or anything glamorous. I'm talking about peace of mind. The agent's team watched our movie and came up with editing suggestions. We listened. Many of their suggestions were good, and we made the changes. But more important than the creative input, they were one big, powerful entity when it came to marketing and sales strategies. It's not like our jobs got easier. They didn't. They got harder, but now we had a sales team that knew our movie, how it would play, and where it could or should be placed.

So in early October we went to work to finish the film (final cut, sound and color correction, transferring to correct formats, and so on) and our agent went to work to get us into the Sundance Film Festival. At this point, we also brought a public relations firm on board. While I thought the PR was something we could do ourselves at first, it wasn't. It's a whole different full-time job and in this business, it's pretty complex. We had a great team that really took care of us.

On Thanksgiving Day we were still waiting to hear from Sundance. I was eating turkey, my cell phone placed at the top of my plate, next to my wineglass. I was waiting to give the toast that never came. Marilyn was sitting by her turkey and cell phone too. Every time my phone rang, I sprang into action. My poor friends and family who called me! It was Thanksgiving, and we were supposed to be thankful for so much, and all I could concentrate on was getting the call.

The call came the Monday after Thanksgiving. We did not get into Sundance. It had been a very long weekend for us. We were really bummed out. Marilyn probably took this hit a little harder than I did. This was her industry, where she had been cutting her teeth for the past decade. Maybe my art and business combo fit well to this work, or maybe I had found my calling, who knows? This was yet to be seen—really (you know what they say, you're only as good as your last project, so maybe I should stop now). But even more, in my "life plans," as everyone tries to think they can plan things, this was never on my list. Riding a Harley and running the New York City marathon are still on my list, but item number ten was never "make a movie." It was basically surreal to me that the words "getting into Sundance" even graced my vocabulary. I had been so proud from the day we bought the camera and started shooting. We made a finished film in less than a year. We had *made* a film.

THE SLAMDANCE FILM FESTIVAL

*A*fter we were rejected by Sundance, we got a call from our agent, who proposed a new strategy. He suggested that we apply to the Slamdance Film Festival, which is held at the same time as Sundance and in the same place, Park City, Utah. The goal was to have a couple screenings to build buzz and then by the third screening they'd try to get all the distributors to come and hope for the best.

We met again to discuss this decision. It was the first time I realized the magnitude of the money invested by my family. It's not an easy place to be. I had to remember those lines from way back when . . . something about doing the movie no matter what! That line was now a little harder to swallow, even though we had come so far. There is something about failing that made me feel that if you are going to fail, it's better to just fail big and fall off the radar. Failing halfway is harder to bear, because there is always the "what if" or the "almost" factor. But really, the only failing here would be financially, as we loved our movie and knew *that* was our true measure of success, regardless of whether it ever made a dime. Money, thought of as a tool, can be paid back, remade, losses rectified. When I got hit with these pockets of anxiety, of doubt, I found it best to ignore them, deny them, to do whatever it took to push them back down, because at that point, there wasn't any turning back. What was I going to do? So forward we went.

There was a lot to be done after we decided to go to Slamdance. The music supervisor and I had to start clearing all the music commercially. Marilyn and I started working on the festival poster and postcards and all the planning for the festival, which would fall at the end of January.

So we buckled down and got busy planning for the festival and finishing the movie. Claudia and I went back and shot some stills of the main "characters" from the film. These two days were a lot of fun because the pressure of "making" the movie was off. We took more than six rolls of film and from there we narrowed it down to about sixteen photos that could either be the poster or a select group that could be a montage on the poster. I had fun sketching possible layouts and eventually everyone in the crew voted and we decided unanimously on the same image—the tango pose of the two kids from Washington Heights.

January rolled around before we knew it. Marilyn and Sabine had been buried in finishing the film. I was getting everything together for the festival, including trying to get a sponsor to pay to have a handful of the kids—one from each school—flown out there with us. They'd be our "stars." We never got that sponsor, but we took the kids anyway, figuring the benefit outweighed the cost. We all arrived in Salt Lake City. The crew stayed in a house we rented in Park City and we treated that as home base. Family and "cast" stayed at a hotel in Salt Lake City and came to the house every day. The kids were ecstatic about staying in a hotel with an indoor pool. My family and the crew's spouses and partners took on various roles to help out, chauffeuring, cooking, hanging posters, and passing out postcards. And we all had so much fun. According to our PR guys, we had the most exclusive party in Park City that year. One night after a huge family-style dinner, we cleared the furniture in the living room of the house and put on our soundtrack. All combinations danced—the kids with the parents, my kids with the PR guys. Everyone! It was a blast. It was at this little party that I realized we were all more a family and less just a group of people thrown together to make a movie. We had such a diverse group, from every walk of life, and here we were, brought together quite un-expectedly, because of one little idea. And we'd be bound for life because of the project—ultimately the most remarkably heartfelt outcome.

Prefestival articles hit the papers. The *Los Angeles Times* movie critic, in the issue everyone and anyone reads on the flights from Los Angeles to Utah, said that the movie to see was not even at Sundance that year but at Slamdance: *Mad Hot Ballroom*. The Park City paper ran a feature on our film. The buzz started. We plastered the city with our posters and even put them all over our big Mad Hot SUV. The kids saw the hard work that was being put into the film. They didn't see Marilyn and me hiring people to do it, they saw us doing it, and our friends and family helping out. It was a lot of work.

We had the first screening of three at the Treasure Mountain Inn at the top of Main Street. There was a problem with the heat during this screening. It was a hundred degrees in the packed room. The whole setup was folding chairs. Amazingly, it was a sold-out show and the film got a standing ovation.

The second screening was in Salt Lake City. It was an interesting old art-house theater, a little rundown. The film projected badly. I felt like wherever or whenever we screened our movie, there was always something wrong or off that would take away from the movie—but we noticed that no one ever left.

The kids and I also handed out postcards and hung posters in the mall, and that was my first hit of the reality that if I had to do this for a year and umpteen more festivals, at my age, I was just going to die. Promoting your film is fun the first night you arrive. After that it's just plain hard, uncomfortable work.

Marilyn and I had some of our own fun experiences too. We went to an out-of-the-way hole-in-the-wall to have a beer with the acquisitions people from Focus Features. It made me realize that all the really important people, the dealmakers, hung out at the normal places that no glam-seeking filmmaker or festival groupies would ever set foot in.

While we were sitting there having a beer with the Focus people, we looked across the room. There were the guys from Roadside Attractions (distributor of *Super Size Me*). When the Focus people left, the Roadside people walked over to us, leaned in, and said, "Ladies . . . you are the belles of the ball! Don't sell that movie too soon!" And we giggled like five-year-old schoolgirls, having no idea what was in store for us.

You have to remember, we were all just kind of normal people thrown into this once-in-a-lifetime experience. This was not something any of us expected, not something any of us thought would ever happen. It was a lot like winning the big prize in the lottery. Even though Marilyn had been working in the industry for years, this catapulting with our movie to the plane of being on distributors' and studio executives' radar was even a long shot for her. And for me, come on, get out of town! We were basically swept off our feet. The "belles of the ball" were really happy with their dance card. There was a united, communal camaraderie and an injection of hope and inspiration to others that this too could happen to them, since it was just happening to us . . . and we were . . . so "normal."

About an hour before the third screening was to begin back at the Treasure Mountain Inn, I sat in the lobby and watched the events unfold. The line to get into the "theater" went down the hall and out the door. Our agent's crew was everywhere—about ten of them—with headphones on and walkie-talkies. They were strategically seating distributors between regular folk, trying to keep one distributor from sitting next to another distributor. Everyone was seriously poker-faced. Distributors don't want to let their competition know they're interested.

Their goal was to *not* have any unnecessary price-driving or, God forbid, have a bidding war ensue.

The screening soon sold out. Our agent's crew had to turn people away. They selectively made sure all the distributors and the press got in. I went out on the Treasure Mountain Inn's balcony because I found the whole scene a bit overwhelming. It was like an out-of-body experience. I could feel that something big was about to go down and, having no frame of reference, I couldn't pinpoint it. My antennae were up and I was extremely emotional, thinking that "my baby" was climbing out of the crib. I found myself wanting to stop all that was happening, to freeze time so that I could let my head and heart catch up, but I had no control. It was absolutely frightening. I know that Marilyn was busy working with the projectionist but she also felt the same pained anxiety. This was, of course, her baby too.

The movie started. The distributors stayed calm, but they typed away on their BlackBerries and quietly made phone calls on their cell phones to their studios' decision makers to get the okay to make an offer. I had a hard time watching it. I stood at the back of the room near the door so that I could go in and out to get some fresh air.

The movie ended and the credits had barely hit the screen when there was a mad rush for the door. Marilyn and I didn't really know what was happening. One of the kids, Michael from Brooklyn, saw the look on my face, got up, and yelled at the audience, "Yous people are being rude!" At that, powerful Hollywood executives brought their stampeding to a stop and then back to a fast tiptoe. They laughed, but anyone who was making a bid was determined to get out of that room and find our sales agent before the next guy did.

Those who were not distributors stayed for the Q&A. Marilyn and I were distracted. Afterward, I can remember that we socialized in the lobby with many people, but our phones kept ringing off the hook. I silenced mine. Marilyn answered every call. At some point in time, our agent called Marilyn and told her to stop answering her phone. He told us that a bidding war was going on over our movie and he would get back to us. A bidding war! We looked at each other, eyes wide.

Our small group went to dinner. Some crew members went to see another movie. By 10 p.m. we were back at the house calling our families. The Mad Hot kids had gone back to the hotel. And then we put on pajamas, poured some wine, and sat there. Sometime after midnight, we got a call from our agent. He told us who the players were and their offers.

What went on for the next six hours was incredible. Doing a big deal in pajamas and "peds" (little footie socks) was great fun, not to mention very surreal. As the night wore on, the number got higher and a few of the players dropped out. One studio wanted us to restructure the film. We didn't want to. They dropped out. Some of the smaller distributors couldn't go any higher than they had already bid, and they left the table. The back and forth of the sporadic wheeling and dealing phone calls continued. What I would have given to be a fly on the wall in those negotiations. Brian did searches on the Internet of the interested studios to see their history of releases and gave us a rundown of each of them—he was like *Distributor Headline News*. We talked about all the movies and whether we liked them, disliked them, how they were marketed (as well as we could remember!), the overall reputation of the studio, and how our movie would fit with them. I was looking for reach and Marilyn was looking for quality and we worked on discussing how to meet in the middle with the choices offered. A couple of higher bids came back and I reminded our agent that there were music, merchandising, and derivative opportunities that should add value. By then, in the wee hours of the morning, everyone else had gone to bed, and Marilyn and I had spent the last couple hours hanging out on the bed staring at each other, eyes wide, as if propped open with toothpicks. I think we were in shock—a little. When the sun came up on January 27 at 6 a.m., the bidding war ended and a final deal was struck. As Marilyn and I lay there with her cell phone to both our ears, pulling it back and forth and back and forth to hear better (we didn't know the cell phone had speaker capability at that point), hearts beating, we said yes to a very generous offer.

When the dust settled, I looked at Marilyn, smiled, winked, and said, "Are we having fun yet?"

*W*hile I'd like to say "and that was that," ending on a high note, it wasn't. From the day we sold the film to the day it premiered in May, we were under the gun to negotiate the rest of the contract and transfer to film and all that came with it. This one last push in postproduction made every other function of the filmmaking process seem like the game of Candyland.

Again, Marilyn's and my team effort was pure, effective synergy. She handled the film transfer and what is known in the industry as deliverables and I handled the legal and business dealings, and we kept each other involved in the other's function so that we could learn and know what to do in the future if one of us should ever get so lucky again.

Reading the list of deliverables (this is a listing of all that a studio will require you to deliver to them and it's all very technical), we first had to find out what everything meant. It was intense. It was a list of more than a hundred items, things to get done, things we didn't understand. Added to that, the studio's deliverables didn't seem to have been updated since maybe the

1940s and many things were outdated with new technology. They were requiring things that didn't exist anymore. It was a strange process and completely overwhelming. We had just made this movie and now there was the equivalent of an extra mountain to climb after getting to the top of the first one. We reviewed this with our production lawyer and then we hired two great postproduction supervisors, who would help to get the job done and done not only right but also in record time.

That description makes what Marilyn had to accomplish sound so basic and one-dimensional. It wasn't. According to Marilyn it was "painful" and "pressurized," even though the two *great* postproduction supervisors were ... well ... great. But there were high moments too. The thrilling part came when she and Claudia and the color timer color corrected each reel. They projected the film and screened it over and over again. And even more awe-inspiring was when Marilyn saw it up on the big screen—*on film*. She thought it so fantastic to *finally* be at this point in the process—to see what the audience would see in theaters. This was the major component of the deliverables. It would be a bore to provide the list of the other hundred-plus items required, but I highly recommend getting a sample deliverables document and giving it a good once-over in advance. If there isn't a final movie yet, at least it'll give you a good jolt and maybe unclog your arteries in the process. But Marilyn advises all new filmmakers *not* to review a deliverables listing in advance because, as she said, "It's hard enough to make a movie let alone know all this horrible stuff comes at the end—but that's me." (Okay, we disagree on one thing.)

The studio contract was also a bear of a document. As we had had a run-in with a big studio the year earlier while in production and while it was scary and quite mind-boggling at the time, it basically helped us know how to deal with the current wheeling and dealing of contract negotiations with our new big studio. Marilyn and I found that it always seems to come down to that age-old conundrum of art vs. commerce—how do you match the two, and who should get what rights? Artists want to keep some level of integrity and the bottom line for the studio is . . . the bottom line. Many of them now are part of big conglomerates and their goal is to increase shareholders' wealth. While the contract wasn't signed until one hour before release, suffice it to say, in the most simplistic way because it *never* really is that simple, that a little horse-trading was done and we all moved on.

With any film, there has to be a commercial marketing angle. I hate to say that because I don't want to put commerce above art, but I think it's true. It's hard to have so much stuff thrown at us in the way of ads, trailers, merchandising, and promotions when a movie is marketed. While it's somewhat of a piece of cake to preach to the art-house crowd who are looking to see good, smart fare no matter what, it's quite another thing to get the rest of the country off their couches and out of their houses, interrupting their already overbusy schedules to get them into the theater to see a movie that is not the latest, greatest blockbuster comedy. As filmmakers, we would've liked to continue with the same promotional angle we had devised during our market and festival days (that now seemed aeons ago) but this is another area where the ball got rolling at the big studio and we had to relinquish a lot of control. We were lucky, though, that the two studio heads at the time were terrific and we got on with them wonderfully. Our poster image, while altered a little, remained basically the same (except our logline was changed—we don't talk about that). We felt these two presidents really liked our film and were quite compassionate about holding our hands and allowing us full access to the whole marketing, sales, and promotion operation.

There was other business to tend to during this last leg of the filmmaking triathlon. Our legal responsibilities until this point consisted of having deal memos and releases. Now, besides the monster studio contract, we had to get our E&O (errors and omissions) insurance approved and activated and we had all the final commercial music contracts to execute and finish. The music clearing process, from beginning to end, would take almost three years. In fact, as of this writing, I'm still waiting for one more signed contract. It was continuous negotiating. Never ending. We had to double all this for another distributor who had bought the rights for only Australia and New Zealand.

And we certainly couldn't forget about funding. Postproduction was going to cost us another $250K (including the extra commercial music costs) and we ended up having to borrow the money (again from family) to finish the film for the studio. Though we would've liked to brush all the other "little" duties under a rug, we couldn't ignore the fact that expenses were still adding up. We had outstanding bills from work done finishing the film for the festival that still had to be paid. Tax season was upon us and it now was very complicated.

Filmmakers just don't have a pile of money fall into their laps. Any eventual box office money is split between the studio and the movie theater owners, so, while the world always sees that number, that money has no effect on the filmmaker's economic living status. The only compensation the filmmakers can count on is the advance. Don't get me wrong, we had an amazing deal. You'd think it was life-changing. But if you do the math, after paying the lawyers, the outstanding bills, postproduction, and the commercial clearing costs of the music, and then paying back loans and the investors along with a rate of return on their money, in our case, we made a decent middle-level management salary, if calculated on an annual basis. If you decide to divide it by the number of hours in a day we put into our project . . . well, we just don't do that. It was truly a labor of love.

The movie premiered at the Tribeca Film Festival in late April 2005. It was a magical evening. I had reached my second goal in the making of this movie—to show it to the kids and their parents (the first goal was paying back investors). The outside "arena" overflowed with people. The Tribeca Film Festival set up an outdoor theater with 2,700 seats and room for thousands more around the periphery and called it the Tribeca "Drive-In." It was right outside the World Financial Center Winter Garden, where the ballroom final competition is held every year, and overlooked the Hudson River with the Statue of Liberty in view. It was estimated by the organization that produces the event that there were more than 3,500 people in attendance. Nothing could beat that night. We had made it that far and anything that would happen afterward would just be icing on the cake.

It was captivating to observe everyone watching the movie. Parents cried. The kids in the movie were in awe that they were watching themselves on the huge screen. After the movie, a few of the TriBeCa kids came up to me and asked if that was the final cut because they didn't like a certain scene, the way they looked, and they'd like to redo it!

This would really be the last time the movie "felt" pure, in its kind of raw essence, on its own. After the event, the movie was released nationwide and the opinions of the film critics were out everywhere. The baby that we created left home, for good, never to look back. It is this moment in time, at the Tribeca Film Festival, that I hold on to most tightly in my memory.

On May 13, 2005, the movie opened in New York City, against *Star Wars: Episode III—Revenge of the Sith.* And so while there were gazillions of young boys and their fathers—and single guys over forty—who would not see our film opening weekend (their loss!), we did have a nice opening that weekend in New York City's two finest art-house theaters. The movie then proceeded to spread out over the country to more than two hundred theaters and turned out to be one of the longest-running contemporary documentaries in movie history, so far. It would be six months before *Mad Hot Ballroom* would play for the last time commercially in a theater.

On October 11, 2005, *Mad Hot Ballroom* hit $8 million in box office sales. And we had climbed up through the top one hundred documentaries of all time, ending up at number seven. *Mad Hot Ballroom* currently ranks in the top ten documentaries of all time.

What was amazing to watch was the grass-roots marketing that seemed to take off on its own. I suppose when you have four minutes of credits that list hundreds of names, and each person in the credits knows twenty people, word spreads like wildfire and people you haven't heard from since third grade are sending notes and e-mails. And because there were no "big" names behind the movie, it became the "little movie that could."

I cannot stress enough the importance of collaboration—everything that had been done, everything that happened, was evidence of this. *Mad Hot Ballroom* would not have been what it was without every single person's input. We wouldn't have had the movie without the idea, without the story, which wouldn't have come about without Pierre Dulaine and his idea of creating and maintaining the program Dancing Classrooms, without the ABrT dance teachers to spread it out, without the New York Public schools having the dance classes, without the principals and teachers wanting the dance classes, without the kids who have to take them, without Carl Glassman of the *Tribeca Trib*, who asked me to follow the TriBeCa team that first year and write the article, without the vision I had when I started to report for that article, without Marilyn's experience as a director and coproducer, without the NYC Department of Education's approving access, without Claudia's cinematic touch and finesse, without Tammy's sound mastery, without Sabine's editing magic, without the money to make the movie so generously provided by my family members, without everyone else who put their hearts and souls into making the film—from our lawyer, music supervisor, postproduction guys, studio heads, and PR guys to the support from "our guys" (Charlie and Brian)—without the amazing "characters" that came out of it—those amazing kids!—and without P.S. 115's winning. Without all this, the movie would not have been what it turned out to be.

It was a toast to the purist definition of independent filmmaking and to the purist definition of documentary filmmaking. It even had a little bit of the heart and essence of pure guerilla filmmaking (and for a mother of twins, now over forty, this was pretty cool). It was a story that went its own course, captured as it unfolded, about regular people, made by regular people, and it succeeded. To newly minted filmmakers out there, knowing that things like this do happen should make you feel pretty good. It should inspire hope. To stay-at-home mothers or fathers of twins or any other combination, to a regular Joe or Jane wanting to change careers, perhaps make a movie, this story could inspire you to try to fulfill your dream.

ACTION PLAN

1. Accept the fact that you will be continuously promoting and marketing your movie. Gear yourself up mentally and stay up on it. Try to have timeless messages so that your efforts can be carried forward throughout the life cycle of your film. Your goal is to sell the film. Salesmanship, if you have it, is another worthy skill in this field.

2. If you can find and secure a producer's rep or sales agent, do so. Their fees vary but they usually work on a commission basis, taking anywhere between 10 percent and 20 percent, depending on if they are handling only the sales aspects of the job or, if you don't already have a lawyer, handling all the transactional paperwork as well. They are obviously more than a big help. Above all, their fee is worth their expertise in strategy and providing peace of mind (which is priceless).

3. Research the studios and other media outlets that are interested in your film: their history of releases, how their films were marketed, and their overall reputation. Think about fit.

4. Get your hands on a list of deliverables (the list of all that a studio will require you to deliver to them) and find out what each item is, familiarizing yourself with the terminology and how to go about getting it done . . . and then hire great postproduction supervisors anyway.

5. Get your hands on a studio contract. Read it and know what everything means.

6. With any film, there has to be a commercial marketing angle. The studio will have to find a way to market your film, which might include changing the one message you worked so hard to put in place. You have to live with the fact that the movie is now, legally and rightfully, their "baby."

7. Our legal responsibilities until this point consisted of having deal memos devised and/or reviewed. We took one and I basically just cut and pasted to make it fit the new job function of a crew member and had our lawyer review it. Other forms, such as releases, can come from the lawyer or you can find generic ones on the Internet and tailor them to your project. Now a whole host of other contracts had to be reviewed by our lawyer: the E&O insurance, final commercial music contracts, and the actual distribution contract and deliverables. Here is where a good relationship with your lawyer is important. Everyone's sleeves are rolled up and all cards are on the table (you hope).

8. Back to the music. It is continuous negotiating. Never ending. Stay up on it because now you are clearing for commercial use, and this is where we watched our music budget expand like a balloon stuck on a helium machine.

9. While all this "front end" promotion and selling is going on, you can't forget about the "back end" support: the

money. Expenses are still coming in and unless you've raised all your money up front, it has to come in from somewhere.

10. If funding is the big picture, then the bookkeeping and accounting is the daily grind. Stay on top of it or it will bury you later. I would throw a month's receipts into a large envelope and then close out that month the following month after all bills were paid. If you can afford it, hire a production bookkeeper to track all your financials.

11. Important fact to know: I made more money on an hourly basis waitressing in college! Independent filmmakers are artists—and their compensation proves this to be true. We were way luckier than most. But the emphasis on "love what you do" gets to the heart of it. It is *so* important to love what you are doing. And that's universal.

15

Epilogue

*F*or those just starting out in the world of filmmaking or those who, like me, have ideas that would make a great movie and are wondering how to get started, put it all together, and get it done, there are ten basic rules that I think are good to keep in mind as you start to invest the time and energy doing one of the hardest things you'll ever do. They essentially apply to everything and anything in life worth doing.

1. *Always* trust your instincts.

2. Know when to hang on and when to let go.

3. Honor your passion by being passionate. It is that simple.

4. Focus! This is 90 percent of it.

5. Time management is an art form. Figure it out and take it to that level.

6. Surround yourself with smart people who will make your project better. It's *all* about collaboration.

7. Stamina! This is the other 90 percent!

8. Know when you need help and where to get it.

9. Be creative and go beyond.

10. Often there is nothing in front of us, only things holding us back, so cut the ropes and leap.

Arts in education. I can't finish without going back to the reason I wanted to make the film in the first place. It is the simple, solid fact that art gives a child room to dream. It's that room to dream that allows children to grow up and think they can do things they might have thought they had no business thinking they could ever do. And so they do them anyway! That also seems to be something that turned out to be true for me. But ultimately, what we all achieved through telling this particular story was and continues to be my big trophy—the trophy I had been going for all along.

I think the crew and everyone else surrounding *Mad Hot Ballroom* felt the same way. First and foremost, we made something we love and are very proud of. It was a wild, amazing ride. Everyone put so much blood, sweat, and tears (yes, tears) and a whole lot of love into this . . . this . . . this giant, massive "thing" whose end result was a simple story told up on the big silver screen. It was good for everyone involved and I would do it again just to create that kind of joy, to see so many get so much out of it, whether that meant happy faces in the audience, new or bigger career opportunities for the crew members, scholarships or acting opportunities for the "cast," or an increase in the number of small feet trotting across gymnasium and cafeteria floors to a Della Reese tune across the country—and around the world.

Mad Hot Ballroom, referred to as a "gift" by many, really turned out to be a gift to me. If I had to say what the greatest thing about the whole journey was, it was that for a short time in *our* lives, these kids bared their souls to us and gave us a rare and special glimpse into their often complicated lives. They let us see the magic that is in each and every one of them— something we all have but often forget about or forget to show. They remind us, and for that, I will be forever grateful.

At the end of *Mad Hot Ballroom*, the principal of P.S. 115 in Washington Heights, Clarita Zeppie, says something that universally applies to everyone—not just the kids in the movie. She says that she tells the kids all the time, "Find something you love to do and do it well." And every time I watch my movie and I hear that line, I listen to her, again and again.

In an e-mail message dated 11/18/2005
8:31:22 a.m. Eastern Standard Time,
New York City Schools Chancellor Joel Klein writes:

It was an inspiring movie—thank you.
I loved the movie. It was full of life and hope and
showed what New York City school kids can
accomplish when they set their minds to it.

> Joel Klein
> Chancellor
> NYC Department of Education

MAD HOT BALLROOM'S AWARDS AND RECOGNITIONS

Best Feature Nomination by the International Documentary Association (IDA)

Best Feature Documentary *and* Best Documentary DVD for the Golden Satellite Awards sponsored by the International Press Association

Heartland's Truly Moving Picture Award for Best Movie by the Heartland Film Festival

The IFP's 15th Annual Gotham Awards honored *Mad Hot Ballroom* with a special Celebrate New York prize

Mad Hot Ballroom received the *Minorities in Business* magazine's 10th Annual Multicultural Prism Award for Outstanding Documentary

Best Documentary at the Karlovy Vary International Film Festival (Czechoslovakia)

The Christopher Award for Best Documentary, whose mission is to encourage people of all ages, and from all walks of life, to use their God-given talents to make a positive difference in the world

The Gabriel Award for Best Documentary, which proclaims a value-centered view of society and humanity and raises the consciousness to focus on what is right and good

New York magazine's 2005 Culture Awards honored *Mad Hot Ballroom* for "Best NYC-made Documentary Your 12-Year-Old Should Be Required to Watch" and "Best Breakout Performances" by both Wilson and Michael

Nominated for Best Documentary
    NAACP Image Awards
    Broadcast Film Critics Choice Awards
    The National Board of Review Motion Picture Awards
    Washington Area Film Critics Awards
    Boston Film Critics Awards
    Toronto Film Critics Awards
    Dallas–Ft. Worth Film Critics Awards
    Chicago Film Critics Awards
    New York Film Critics Awards
    Los Angeles Film Critics Awards
    International Press Academy
    Young Artist Award
    Overseas Envelope Critics

Official Selection
    Tribeca Film Festival
    Slamdance Film Festival
    Berlin International Film Festival
    Seattle Film Festival
    Bermuda Film Festival
    CineVegas
    San Francisco International Film Festival
    Maui Film Festival
    Phoenix Film Festival

Audience Award for Best Film
    Cleveland Film Festival
    Chicago International Documentary Film Festival
    Philadelphia Film Festival
    Malibu Film Festival

The Oscar Short List
    One of fifteen chosen out of eighty-two documentaries in 2005

American Ballroom Theater's Dancing Classrooms is currently in more than two hundred New York City public schools, and numerous other public school systems across the country and around the world.

Appendix A: Mad Hot *Ballroom* Timeline

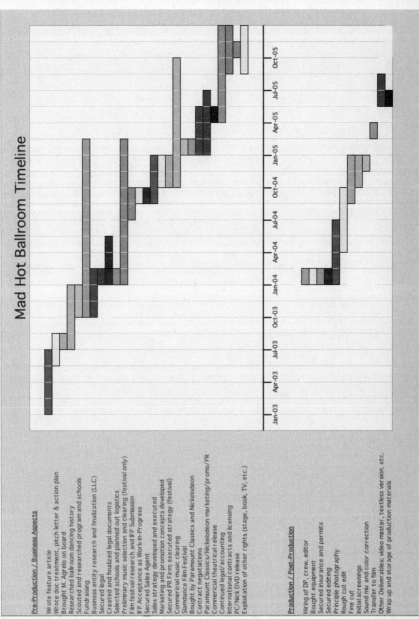

Mad Hot Ballroom Timeline

Pre-Production / Business Aspects

Wrote feature article
Wrote doc treatment, pitch letter & action plan
Brought M. Agrelo on board
Researched ballroom dancing history
Scouted and researched program and schools
Fundraising
Business entity research and finalization (LLC)
Secured legal
Created and finalized legal documents
Selected schools and planned out logistics
Preliminary music selection and clearing (festival only)
Film festival research and IFP Submission
IFP Acceptance as Work-in-Progress
Secured Sales Agent
Sales strategy developed and executed
Marketing and promotion concepts developed
Secured PR Firm; executed strategy (festival)
Commercial music clearing
Siamdance Film Festival
Contract negotiations
Bought by Paramount Classics and Nickelodeon
Paramount Classics/Nickelodeon marketing/promo/PR
Commercial theatrical release
Continued legal/accounting
International contracts and licensing
PC/Nick DVD release
Exploitation of other rights (stage, book, TV, etc.)

Production / Post-Production

Hiring of DP, crew, editor
Bought equipment
Secured insurance and permits
Secured editing
Principle photography
Rough cut edit
Fine cut
Initial screenings
Sound mix and color correction
Transfer to film
Other Deliverables; video master, textless version, etc.
Wrap up and storage of production materials

169

Appendix B

Recommended Reading
(in order of relevance to the filmmaking process)

Alan Rosenthal, *Writing, Directing and Producing Documentary Films and Videos* (Third Edition). Carbonsville and Edwardsville, IL. Southern Illinois University Press. © 1990, 1996, 2002 by Alan Rosenthal.

Morrie Warshawski, *Shaking the Money Tree: How to Get Grants and Donations for Film and Television* (Second Edition). Studio City, CA. Published by Michael Wiese Productions. © 2003 Morrie Warshawski.

Louise Levison, *Filmmakers and Financing: Business Plans for Independents* (Third Edition). Massachusetts. Focal Press. © 2001 Louise Levison.

Michael C. Donaldson, *Clearance & Copyright: Everything the Independent Filmmaker Needs to Know* (Second Edition). Los Angeles, CA. Silman-James Press. © 2003 Michael C. Donaldson.

Deke Simon and Michael Wiese, *Film & Video Budgets* (Third Edition). Studio City, CA. Published by Michael Wiese Productions. © 2001 Deke Simon and Michael Wiese.

Jon M. Garon, *The Independent Filmmaker's Law and Business Guide: Financing, Shooting and Distributing Independent and Digital Films*. Chicago, IL. Published by A. Cappella Books. An imprint of Chicago Review Press, Inc. © 2002 Jon M. Garon.

Chris Gore, *The Ultimate Film Festival Survival Guide* (Second Edition). Hollywood, CA. IFILM and Lone Eagle Publishing Company. © 2001 Chris Gore.

Mad Hot Ballroom *"Clutch" Glossary*

*I*t was hard to mention all the crew and industry names in the book and keep the flow. Therefore, I'd like to list those people mentioned in the book either by name or just by professional description who were totally clutch in the success of *Mad Hot Ballroom*. Thank you!

Director   Marilyn Agrelo

Director of Photography   Claudia Raschke-Robinson

Editor   Sabine Krayenbühl

Production Sound Mixer   Tammy M. Douglas

Executive Producers   Phyllis Sewell
                                     Charles Sewell
                                     Daphne and Richard Ottens
                                     Sylvia Mellman

Line Producer   Brian David Cange

Associate Producer   W. Wilder Knight II

Original Music by	Steven Lutvak and Joseph Baker
Original Song Performed by	Tina Fabrique
Music Supervisor	Mark Reynolds
Postproduction Supervisors	Mike Jackman Stuart McPhee
"The Big Studio" Contact	Arianna Bocco
Distribution Advisory Services	Cinetic Media John Sloss Micah Green Dan Steinman The Whole Cinetic Team
Former Paramount Presidents	David Dinerstein Ruth Vitale
The Whole Paramount Team	
Publicity	TC:DM & Associates David Magdael Winston Emano Steven Wallace Anne Stulz

Carl Glassman, *The Tribeca Trib*

The City of New York
Mayor's Office of Film,
Theatre and Broadcasting

IFP New York

NYC Department of Education
Chancellor Joel Klein

Dancing Classrooms—a project
   of American Ballroom Theater
Pierre Dulaine, Codirector
Yvonne Marceau, Codirector
All the ABrT Teaching Artists,
   especially Rodney Lopez, Victoria
   Malvagno, and Alex Tchassov.

P.S.115	Washington Heights, Manhattan
Teacher	Yomaira Reynoso
Principal	Clarita Zeppie
P.S. 150	TriBeCa, Manhattan
Teacher	Allison Sheniak
Principal	Alyssa Polack
P.S. 112	Bensonhurst, Brooklyn
Teacher	Leslie Freij
Principal	Louise Verdemare
P.S. 144	Forest Hills, Queens
Teacher	Terri Mintzer
Director of Arts	Lois Olshan
Principal	Susan Bahaloul

And last but never least . . . all the kids!

Francisco A. Infante

*A*my Sewell is working on a television sit-com called *Mommy Juice*, as well as her next documentary, which she plans to release in 2008. She established and manages a public nonprofit organization, Give It Up for the ARTS!, with the primary goal of helping kids in need who have an interest in the arts to further their education. She lives in New York City with her husband, a teacher and coach, and her daughters, who keep her well supplied with comic material.